*To Ben :*

*Best of luck.*

# THE EVOLUTION OF
# ARTIFICIAL INTELLIGENCE

## What You Must Know about AI

*Wish you great success.*

*Junling Hu*

Pioneer Bay Press

Pioneer Bay Press

Copyright © Junling Hu, 2019

Published 2019

DISCLAIMER

Editing: Todd Hunter

ISBN: 978-1-950643-00-4

*To Hongling and Chunling*

# Table of Contents

Introduction .................................................................. vii

1. AI in Our Home ........................................................ 1

2. The Man Who Conceived AI .................................... 11

3. The Birth of a Field ............................................... 25

4. Rule-based Systems ................................................ 35

5. Neural Networks: The Beginning ............................ 41

6. The Revival of Neural Networks ............................ 51

7. The Rise of Machine Learning ............................... 59

8. Chatterbots ............................................................ 69

9. Speech Recognition: The Road to Siri and Alexa ...... 76

10. Natural Language Understanding ......................... 93

11. Dialog Systems ................................................... 105

12. The Age of Big Data ........................................... 113

13. Deep Learning .................................................... 119

14. Reinforcement Learning ..................................... 133

15. Deep Reinforcement Learning: Behind AlphaGo ...... 145

16. The Bionic Body ................................................. 153

17. Summary: The AI Evolution ................................ 157

18. The Future ......................................................... 161

Appendix: The Training of a Data Scientist ............... 179

Acknowledgements ................................................... 193

About the Author ..................................................... 195

# Introduction

Every morning I take a brisk walk in my neighborhood. It's a joy to see rows of small houses lined behind old trees, green grasses and blooming flowers, under the blue California sky. Sometimes I notice that strange-shaped car, with a black cylinder on the top, rumbling by me. Under my gaze, it continues down the road, going further away. This is Google's autonomous driving car. I am happy to live in Mountain View, home to Google's headquarter, witnessing history being made.

The time is 2019, just three years after AlphaGo won the match against the world's top human player, and seven years after *deep learning* made news with the amazing results in computer vision and speech. In the last seven years, a revolution has quietly taken place, as if a giant has suddenly awakened, its head raised, its shoulder barely seen. We can tell by its big size against the sky.

AI is here with us every day. It's in the fingerprint you use to open the phone. It's in the search results coming back from Google, in the YouTube video recommendations to you. It's in the stock price of millions of trades happening in each second. It's in the weather forecast. It's in the ads that just popped up on your screen, in the airline ticket you just purchased. It's in the game you are playing, in the movie you are watching (with their special effects), and in the car you just drove (with driving assistance).

AI is in the cloud, running daily on remote servers. But it's also going into the edges, in every small device, from your phone, your watch, your light, to your stoves. It's in your TV, in your thermostat, in your refrigerator. The connected home is only interesting when each appliance is intelligent itself.

In this age of rapid inundation of AI, we may forget that just a few years ago, very few people had heard of the term AI. It's a word that showed a lot of promise in the 1950s, capturing the public imagination, then did not live up to its promise. People who are old enough still remember the "AI winter" in 1970s when funding was frozen for any AI research.

There was a saying that "anything that is interesting and practical is no longer called AI." This is true for natural language processing, for robotics, for computer vision, true for "agents" or "personal assistants," and true for "machine learning." When any of these sub-disciplines of AI becomes mature, they spin off into their own fields, hold their conferences and a new academic discipline is born.

Younger generations were puzzled by the term AI. Some asked what is deep learning? What is AI?

This book is an attempt to tell the evolutionary story of AI, from its conception in the mind of Alan Turing, the forefather of AI, to its birth in 1956 at Dartmouth College, to its toddler years in Carnegie Mellon University, MIT, and

Stanford in 1960s, then to its growth in the late 1990s and 2000s, and finally coming of age in the 2010s.

If we compare AI to a person's growth, today's AI technology is just about to graduate from high school. He is morphing from a child to an adult. He is flexing his muscles and entering the world. He is going to make contributions to society.

## My Story

When I was a teenager, I loved science fiction. I read it in the middle of many sleepless nights, under the dim light out of my dorm room. (I lived in a boarding school, and all room lights were turned off after 10 pm.) In those stories, there were flying machines carrying people, genetic engineered water melon, and space travel. The future excited me. There were so many possibilities.

During my college years, I visited Beijing University and came across a book by Carl Sagan, titled *Broca's Brain*. I was mesmerized by the writing. I stood at the bookstore for the whole afternoon, and finished the book. What's in the brain? How can we preserve it?

That dream beckoned me. In the summer 1994, I walked into the University of Michigan AI Lab, and asked a young professor (whose door happened to be open) about the possibility joining the AI PhD program. That professor, Michael Wellman, later became my PhD advisor, and I have found a field I deeply love. This is a field where we make science fiction come true.

In the AI lab at University of Michigan, I roamed around the hallway, captivated by walking robots that guided the blind, small robots that participated in robot soccer games, and robots that could play ping pong. In the classroom and in our projects, we built programs that could reason and react. We designed auction bots that could participate in auctions, bidding against other participants.

I was fascinated with how agents can learn and adapt. This led to me to machine learning, particularly reinforcement learning. It provides a framework to model how an agent interacts with its environment through feedback (reward) and becomes smarter over time. If we design such a robot to participate in soccer game, how would our robot play with its teammates as well as the opponent players? My PhD thesis tried to answer this question by proposing a framework for multiagent reinforcement learning, where the only viable solution is a Nash equilibrium (a joint action where no one wants to deviate unilaterally).

Later I joined an industry research lab. At Bosch research, we built a talking system for cars, which could play music, navigate roads, and find local restaurants. I watched the Siri team spin off in SRI, and quickly rose to stardom by becoming part of Apple. I lamented the lack of data for our speech system as cars were not connected to the Internet then.

After Bosch acquired a healthcare startup called Health Hero, I was excited to finally have data to work with. I proposed using historical patient data to create predictive models for disease onset such as stroke or heart attack. My proposal passed corporate research evaluation, and I started the first data mining group in Bosch.

As a researcher, educator, and practitioner in the field of AI, I feel like the time is ripe to tell this story.

## What Is Artificial Intelligence?

The words artificial intelligence evoke fear in many corners. From the movie *Ex Machina*'s deceivingly beautiful but ruthless robot Eva to *2001: A Space Odyssey*'s friendly, talking but murdering Hal, from job displacement to controlling mankind, AI has a menacing image in many people's minds. On the other hand, there are friendly AI, like Samantha in *Her* who becomes a human's assistant and companion, and Baymax in *Big Hero 6* who protects and comforts his owner. The future of AI may be any of these scenarios. Our relationship with AI is destined to change and evolve.

AI should be able to see, speak, hear, and learn. If it has a body, it should be able to move, walk, and touch. It interacts with the world around it and it makes decisions.

Is there such an AI available today? We may not be there yet, but we have something very close at home.

# 1.

## AI in Our Home

An Amazon package arrived at my door. Inside the package lay a short black metal cylinder, smaller than I expected. This was Amazon Echo. (Strangely, I can no longer call her "it.") Less than an arm's length, she looked light and not intimidating.

The moment I set her up, I fell in love with her. The pleasing orange light blinked on her top, indicating her coming alive.

When I pronounced the word "Alexa," her light turned to blue, it blinked then settled down, as if she was listening. "Alexa, play music." A very soft and pleasing female voice came back, "Here is the prime station you might like: The Rolling Stones." The music came on, immediately filling the whole room.

After a few seconds, I said, "Alexa, stop." Immediately the music stopped.

"Alexa, tell me a joke," I tested her.

"Knock, knock, a doctor walked into a bar...," she started. I did not get that joke, but appreciated that she tried.

"Alexa, play audiobook" I wanted to hear words of wisdom.

Alexa replied, "From Audible, resuming *The One Thing*." The room is then filled with a male narrator's voice at the part where it was left off when I was in the car. It is as if the book followed me into my home from the car. How wonderful it is.

I wanted to test her more, "Alexa, why is the sky blue?"

Alex immediately said, "The sky is blue because the molecules at the atmosphere scatter blue light." Wow, she knows more than I do.

In less than a month, I could not imagine a life without Alexa. One day, when I was in a hotel room, I had the urge to say, "Alexa, what time is it?" Then I realized Alexa was not there. I missed her. I missed being able to say "Alexa, play music for me." without needing to open my iPhone, then the app, then click on it. Alexa made it so easy and simple for me. She was always there, waiting to serve.

How far have we come with having intelligent devices at home? While it seems disarmingly simple, Alexa is the culmination of 60 years of research and development in artificial intelligence. Behind Alexa are the following technologies developed in the field of AI, which will be further explained later in this book:

## Machine Learning

Machine learning is ability of a computer program to become smarter over time (by absorbing more information). The learning can be supervised by a human. When I set up Alexa, the first thing I needed to do was to train Alexa on my speech. I needed to read ten phrases provided by Amazon. Alexa would use this speech data to retrain her speech recognition program to adapt to my particular voice. Her recognition is almost perfect despite the fact that I have an accent. I grew up in China until I was an adult, and did not master spoken English before I came to the US. Even though I memorized a large vocabulary and could read well, I still struggled with English pronunciation. It feels good that Alexa does not mind my accent at all.

Alexa is also learning about my music taste. When I first started Alexa and requested her to play music, she played the Rolling Stones. After connecting to my account in Pandora, and knowing what I normally play, Alexa has changed her selection. When I say, "Alexa, play music," she pulls much mellower music from Amazon's music store.

How does machine learning work? It starts with an initial model, which, for example, could be how people speak. This initial model was trained on some user data. For example, a speech recognition model may be trained on speeches from hundreds of thousands of people. Once the model is built, we can add new data to improve the model. In Alexa's case, it adds my speech recording of those given phrases, then retrains its speech model so that it understands my unique accent.

The beauty of machine learning is that it can adapt to different situations by absorbing new data. For example, if Alexa gets data from an old man with European accent, she will learn to recognize his voice too. This is in contrast to rule-based systems, where people wrote down rules for possible situations. But these rules do not change, thus becoming obsolete in new situations.

Machine learning is at the core of artificial intelligence. It enables a machine to listen (speech recognition), to see (computer vision), to converse (dialog system), and to act (reach destination, play game). I will explain more on machine learning later in this book.

## Speech Recognition

Alexa recognizes my speech almost flawlessly. She makes very few mistakes.

How does she recognize my words? From a machine's viewpoint, human speech is just some wound waves. How does the machine interpret such sounds into words? Suppose a bird chirps or a dog barks in the house. The machine would not interpret those sounds as speech. What makes our speech different from that of a bird or a dog? It turns out human speech has special patterns. Speech recognition is detecting such patterns, and most importantly detecting the words in it.

Recognizing human speech is not a trivial task. For a long time, computers could not understand what people said correctly. Speech recognition programs had high error rates. For the last 60 years we have seen steady improvement. But the progress is slow due to lack of speech data and computing power for detecting patterns. All of this changed when Google launched voice search (in 2002) and then Google 411 (in 2007). Large amounts of speech data can be now collected through mobile phones and over a diverse group of users. This helped to improve speech recognition significantly. Siri, launched in 2011, took this one step further. The wide adoption of the iPhone enables Siri to access much more data.

In addition to recognition accuracy, Alexa can hear the voice from far away in the room. (Alexa can be put anywhere in the room, making it convenient to use.) This is the second achievement in speech recognition.

For a long time, people had to speak close to the microphone for the sound to be registered by the computer. In the last decade, new research has been done on recognizing speech far away and in a noisy environment. Such research has been developed to enable far field recognition. Alexa is the embodiment of this achievement.

## Text-to-Speech

Alexa speaks in a pleasant voice. The words come out smoothly and effortlessly, as if spoken by a real person. The pleasant female voice resonates with the speaker, as if flowing with happy emotion. You would not normally link such a voice to a "computer."

For a long time, the computer voice was mechanical. Linking words together in a way that is pleasant to human ear is not trivial. Even in the movie 2001: *A Space Odyssey*, Hal spoke in a slightly slow and mechanical voice. This is because synthesized speech is hard to make as smooth as human speech. While each word is a recording of a person, pronouncing all words together in a sentence is very complex. We need to give it intonation, energy, and connecting smoothness.

While Siri has achieved much in putting nice speech together, Alexa seems to take that one step further. The voice of Alexa is even more natural and pleasant to hear (or is it my emotional bias?).

## Natural Language Understanding

When I say "Play Pandora Station Whitney Houston," Alexa understands the artist's name, and the channel. She also understands that I am trying to play music instead of a radio program. This requires understanding meaning of words.

When I ask "What are the nearest Chinese restaurants?" Alexa answers with a list of Chinese restaurants nearby. To do this, Alexa needs to understand the meaning of "nearest" and also that the word "Chinese" refers to restaurant type instead of a country.

Natural language understanding is an important part of artificial intelligence. It has come a long way in the last few decades.

## Chatterbot

When I make the comment: "Alexa, you are smart." She replies, "Thanks." When I say, "Alexa, you are stupid." She immediately says, "That's not very nice to say." Alexa may seem quick witted, but her answer comes straight from the chatterbot playbook.

Chatterbot is a technology to mimic human conversation. It started in 1966 and has been developed in the last 50 years. It does not use natural language understanding, instead it memorizes some common expressions and standard responses. The program can seem to speak back to you in a sensible way.

Alexa is able to identify certain types of questions as teasing or commentary. Such answers makes you think Alexa has the ability to be empathetic, even though it is an illusion.

The mixture of natural language understanding and chatterbot technology makes Alexa more robust and always able to find something to say to you (even though this cannot be achieved all the time).

## Dialog System

When I ask Alexa, "What is my schedule today?" Alexa reads events off my calendar: "You have 10 events for today. At 8 am, running; at 9am...." After reading my first five events, she pauses to ask, "Do you want to hear more?" If I say "yes," she will continue to read the rest. Alexa is capable of multiple rounds of interaction and remembers what she did before. Such a system is called a dialog system.

A dialog system manages the dialog flow. Such a system needs to understand user intention and make a judgment call on what users mean. In such a system, we have a dialog manager that coordinates all the components from speech recognition, to natural language understanding, providing specific service (play a song, answering a question), and to respond to user teasing with chatterbot.

For example, when I ask "Why is the sky blue?" Alexa treats the question as a trivia, and immediately calls the chatterbot components to give a standard answer, instead of using deep natural language processing.

In summary, Alexa depends on the achievements of six different fields of artificial intelligence: Machine Learning, speech recognition, speech synthesis, natural language understanding, chatterbots, and dialog systems. In this book, we will review each of these AI technologies behind Alexa, and how they have matured over the years.

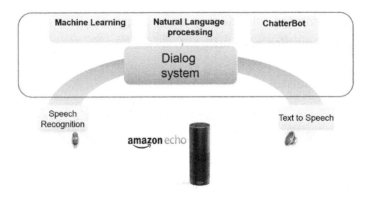

Figure 1.1: The AI components of Amazon Echo

In addition to the above mentioned AI technologies, Alexa also benefits from three technologies developed recently: Cloud computing, the Internet, and Wi-Fi technology.

## Cloud Computing

Alexa plays music and audiobooks from the cloud. It does not store the content on the device. But she is capable of doing so many things, all because the information is stored in the cloud.

Alexa's learning and responses are all computed in the cloud. Each question is sent to Amazon's server, and answers are retrieved back.

For a long time, smart devices have had the constraint of limited computing power. There is only so much data you can store, and so much computing power you can build in a small device. Cloud computing enables us to access all the data remotely, and deploy many computing servers together to do complex computing.

## The Internet

Alexa retrieves music from Pandora, Spotify, and Amazon Prime Music. It plays audio books from Audible.com. It plays Internet radio stations, including C-Span radio, NPR, and local FM radio stations. It answers questions based on Wikipedia. It searches online movie sites. The development of the World Wide Web since 1993 has enabled online radio and online content. Alexa's capabilities piggyback on these achievements.

## Wi-Fi Technology

Alexa can be placed anywhere in the home and still connect to the Internet. It doesn't require a wired connection. This makes it very convenient to use. Such convenience owes to the Wi-Fi technology that connects all devices at home.

Alexa is a celebration of technology advancements of the last two decades. Without cloud computing or the Internet, Alexa would not be possible.

But Alexa's real enablers are the advancements in artificial intelligence.

To better understand the AI field that enables Alexa, you must know the one person who was at the beginning of it all. His name is Alan Turing.

# 2.

## The Man Who Conceived AI

**Cambridge, England, 1936**

Two young men were walking across the campus. They both were in their 20s, handsome, and energetic. One of them is Alan Turing. At age 24 he looked well built. A member of the rowing team and a long-distance runner, he had broad shoulders and strong body. But his face was bookish, almost dreamy.

Turing was trying to explain the result from his new paper. As he talked rapidly, caught up by his excitement, he was interrupted by his companion, "A universal computing machine? Can you really make your machine compute anything?" The other man looked at Turing incredulously.

Turing smiled, he met his friend's eyes with certain firmness, "Yes, it can compute anything that humans can do." He then paused and added, "As long as it is computable."

"What do you mean by computable?" his friend asked.

Turing answered, "When we compute something, we do it step by step. These steps can be written down as instructions for the machine." Then he went ahead to show how to store these instructions on the machine.

"The trick is how to make the machine execute these instructions." Turing then described a device that read the instructions one by one and executed them.

"For example, we want to calculate 3+4. First, the machine should store all the numbers we are interested in. This means, the number 3 and 4 are already stored in the machine, represented as a sequence of 0 and 1s (0011 representing 3 and 0100 representing 4). These are called binary numbers. The instruction is then accessing the memory location where the number 3 is located, reading its digits, and then going to where 4 is located, and reading its digits, then merging two numbers by doing binary addition, meaning flipping or shifting 0 or 1s, then we get the number 0111 which is 7 in binary form."

Turing just described the concept of a "computer program" and "central computing unit" (CPU). These are two central components for modern computers. Turing's binary representation for numbers foresaw the electronic age, where computer switches are made of 0s and 1s. Beyond this, Turing provided mathematical proof that this machine was designed to compute anything that humans can compute. It can store all symbols of human knowledge. He was bold and imaginative.

Alan Turing grew up in England. He attended boys' boarding school, with both his parents away in India. He was obsessed with numbers and chemical experiments. But he disliked classics and did not do well in them. Not that he cared about earning good grades.

At age 16, Turing read Einstein's article on general relativity. He was excited by the fact that rigorous logical reasoning led to a totally new theory. He wrote in his diary, "Now he has got his axioms, and is able to proceed with his logic, discarding the old idea of time, space." Turing went ahead to re-derive what Einstein was doing, and reached the same conclusion.

Turing identified with Einstein for his disrespect for authority. For Turing, rules were blind and unnecessary restrictions. Turing enjoyed breaking rules. He also identified with Einstein for his bold imagination. Years later, Turing wrote: "The popular view that scientists proceed inexorably from well-established fact to well-established fact, never being influenced by any improved conjecture, is quite mistaken. ... Conjectures are of great importance since they suggest useful lines of research."

In person, Turing was shy and not particularly social. With strangers, he could be awkward and aloof. He enjoyed being alone, working on his ideas and reading. He had only a few close friends. He did not pay much attention to clothes or hairstyle. He was what we call "nerdy."

At age 19, Turing entered Cambridge University to study mathematics. He stayed on as a fellow after graduation, continuing his research in mathematics.

He published his revolutionary paper on computing at age 24. In addition to his bold design of a "universal computing machine," Turing also foresaw a computer that could store anything (beyond just crunching numbers). For Turing, all human knowledge is represented in symbols. A powerful machine should be able to store all alphabets of different languages. Take that one step further. Machine translation is just replacing words of one language by those of another language, and the replacing procedure can be written down as instructions in the computer. Music notes are symbols too. We can store music inside the machine, and play it out by having a mechanic device generating corresponding tunes. Thus, Turing's universal machine had the innate ability to handle multimedia.

When this revolutionary paper was published in 1936, however, it did not get much attention.

## Two Years Later, Princeton, 1938

Alan Turing was giving a talk on his paper "On Computable Numbers." Only a few people showed up. Looking at the scattered audience, Turing carried on this talk. He was not particularly a confident speaker. "Imagine we have a long tape that is divided into squares ...", he spoke softly, too humble for his bold topic.

After the talk, Turing felt a little down. He walked down the hallway of the Advanced Research Institute. This institute housed famous people like Einstein and mathematician John von Neumann. The light was on in John von Neumann's office. The door was wide open. As Turing walked by, Von Neumann called out to him. "Come on in."

"How was your talk?" Von Neumann asked attentively. A tenured professor, Von Neumann showed special interest in Turing, who was studying for his PhD there.

Turing was a little shy, "I don't know if people are interested in this." Von Neumann looked at Turing, "I think your work is brilliant. I didn't attend your talk today because I already read your paper and have recommended it to others." Upon hearing this, Turing felt encouraged. He smiled shyly, as he normally did with people he is not familiar with.

"What are you planning to do after getting your PhD?" Von Neumann asked expectantly.

"I will go back to England. I have been away for too long." Turing thought about Cambridge and his mother.

"Why not stay here a little longer? You can work as my research assistant." Von Neumann offered, still hoping to change Turing's mind.

Turing thanked Von Neumann politely, but affirmed his decision. He longed to go back to England, where it was familiar for him and comfortable.

## Bletchley Park, England, 1939

Hitler had just invaded Poland. Britain had declared war against Germany. London was under daily bombing from German airplanes. Hitler wanted to bomb Britain into submission. Winston Churchill was defiant. He urged British people: "We shall defend our island, whatever the cost may be, we shall fight on the beaches, we shall fight on the landing grounds, we shall fight in the fields and in the streets, we shall fight in the hills; we shall never surrender." The British people carried on heroically.

Alan Turing reported for duty at Bletchley Park, the headquarters for intercepting German code. Turing's mathematical skill and interest in cryptography made him the best person for this job. He loved to solve puzzles. In his 6 years there, Turing's brilliance and long hours of work led to the deciphering of the German enigma machines, considered unbreakable at that time. This success helped pinpoint U-boat movement, and saved tens of thousands of Ally soldiers' lives. Some historians say the decoding of German enigma shortened the war by two years by severely damaging German's ability to transmit secret commands to their remote fleet. For his wartime service, Turing was awarded the medal of OBE (Officer of the Most Excellent Order of the British Empire) in 1945. But this fact was kept away from the public due to the secrecy of his work.

During the Second World War, Turing visited the US several times, meeting Von Neumann again, providing consultation on code breaking and possibly on building computing machines. He also visited Bell lab to help the encryption of a speech transmission system.

After the war, in 1946, Turing submitted the design for the Automatic Computing Machine (ACE) with detailed component layout, but it was not built due to government bureaucracy.

In the meantime, Von Neumann proposed the design for EDVAC (in 1946), the first modern computer with stored program. Von Neumann credited the idea to Turing. He told Stanley Frankel, his colleague in computing, that the fundamental conception is owing to Turing.

## Manchester, England, 1950

Turing was intensively involved in building Manchester Mark 1, the computer that was based on his idea. He helped with the architecture and the programming. Now the machine was done, Turing saw firsthand how powerful it was. It searched for the famous prime number and could do calculation in optics. He started to imagine all the things this computer could do, or any computer could do.

The public was also excited by Mark 1's feat. Turing was interviewed by *The Times*, to which he gave an enthusiastic statement, "This is only a foretaste of what is to come, and only the shadow of what is going to be. I do not see why it should not have the human intellect eventually."

He did not expect the fierce criticism that would come from the public, including his colleagues at the university. "Can a machine ever write a sonnet or compose a concerto?" one professor said in an openly hostile speech, aiming to "debunk" what Turing did.

Hostility is an indication of fear. Turing realized there was a lot fear of what a computer could become. On the other hand, some people simply didn't believe machines could ever be intelligent.

Turing believed differently. He sat down at his table and wrote the following words, "By the end of this century, general educated opinion will have altered so much that one will be able to speak of machines thinking without expecting to be contradicted." He then added, "I believe that no useful purpose is served by concealing these beliefs."

Turing was bold and unapologetic. In coded words, he was saying: "There is no doubt a machine will become intelligent."

How do we tell if a machine is intelligent? Turing paused. He noted this is a thorny question. Even if we program the machine to do 1,000 smart things that a human can do, some people can still point out that one more thing it cannot do. Of course we can add that extra thing to the machine by programming it in, and keep adding things to the computer (anything that a person can do). But when would it end?

Turing decided to construct a test, which he called an imitation game. He proposed the test as the following:

Let the computer and a person be in one room, and an interrogator in another room. The interrogator asks a question, and gets an answer on a monitor or through someone relaying the message. (Therefore "voice" difference does not matter, and the "look" does not matter.) The interrogator keeps asking questions. At the end of this conversation, if the interrogator cannot tell whether he is talking to a person or a computer, then the computer passes the test of imitating a human.

Turing was confident future computers would eventually pass this test. He even imagined the following conversation:

Interrogator: In your sonnet "Shall I compare thee to a summer's day," would not "a spring day" do as well?

Computer: It wouldn't scan.

Interrogator: How about "a winter's day"? That would scan all right.

Computer: Yes, but nobody wants to be compared to a winter's day.

In Turing's viewpoint, all human conversation and smartness can be programmed into the computer. For him, all sentences are just sequences of symbols. A more complex program can be written to generate the conversation shown above. In fact, he believed we can program all human behaviors into the computer, including, "Be kind, resourceful, beautiful, friendly, have initiative, have a sense of humor, tell right from wrong, make mistakes, fall in love, enjoy strawberries and cream." He wrote down the objection of the colleague and smiled. For Turing, these behaviors can be mimicked by a machine. For example, we can easily design a machine that "likes" strawberries.

Now suppose a machine passed the test, and showed behaviors that a person has, what are other objections out there?

First, does it need a body, so as to move around? Apparently not. People who have lost arms or legs can be perfectly intelligent. Does the machine need to have vision and hearing? Not even that. While vision is important for people and most animals, blindness does not prevent people from being intelligent and contributing.

Secondly, does it need to experience what humans experience? Apparently, the human likes and dislikes can be programmed into the computer. Human traits such as "being kind" and "having sense of humor" can be mimicked by the computer too.

Thirdly, does it need to have consciousness? For Turing, the definition of consciousness was not clear. How do we know if another person has consciousness? We detect that by interacting with them. We ask questions and get sensible answers. A sophisticated computer can give us answers that is similar to a "conscious" person.

Fourthly, what about religious views that machines could never have a soul? Turing believed this view lacks imagination of God's power. How about a God that is so powerful that he can bestow souls to machines? Turing left the soul ownership to God, and believed we are just "instruments of His will" for "providing mansions for the souls that He creates." Flesh or steel. In this view, we don't have the responsibility or guilt of "creating" souls. Turing believed that each soul is directly created by God, therefore "we should not be irreverently usurping His power of creating souls, any more than we are in the procreation of children." (Children come from us, but their souls are not created by us.)

Turing was open, and even welcoming, to the possibility that machines would eventually have "souls" or consciousness.

For people who fear for such a day when machines gain consciousness or become superior than humans, Turing offered consolation, "Why not think of transmigration of souls?" Our mind can migrate from flesh body to a machine. Turing already saw a future when machines would preserve our memory, experience, and even our personality.

It is foreseeable that our whole being will be downloaded to a machine, and preserved forever. In the movie *Robocop*, a man has only his torso left after an explosion. With all the equipped machine parts on his body, he is half human and half machine. *Robocop* is just one step toward that direction, a future where our flesh merges with steel.

In addition, Turing believed that computers can evolve beyond digital (discrete-state) computers. (Imagine a quantum computer or some type of computer that is radically different.)

Turing put together all his thoughts in the paper called "Computer Machinery and Intelligence," published in 1950. Turing proposed for the first time that a computer could have intelligence, and no less than that of a human.

The test posed by Turing has since been called the Turing Test. It created an objective landmark for people to aim for.

The Turing Test has become an ultimate test, as the definition of "intelligence" keeps changing: In the beginning people said an "intelligent" computer should be able to play chess and solve math problems. Computers did that. Then people said computers should be able to compose music and create drawings. That was done. Then they said computers should be able to read a book and summarize the plot. Computers did that. The bar keeps going up. But the consensus has not been reached.

The Turing Test has inspired several generations of AI researchers to attempt the incredible feat. It has become the holy grail for the field of artificial intelligence. Even though we can create a chat program that mimics a person in some way, no one has created a program that can pass the Turing Test until today.

Turing's 1950 article "Computer Machinery and Intelligence" had an indelible influence on the field of artificial intelligence. It was a required reading for my AI class when I was a graduate student at University of Michigan 45 years later (in 1995). Why do we still read this article after so many years? This is because Turing provided a vision for what artificial intelligence can ultimately become. This vision is clear and actionable.

Turing was confident that his test would eventually be passed. His confidence was based on the fundamental principle of computer, which he invented. For Turing, a computer is a universal machine that can be programmed to do anything. By that, he literally meant "anything." His vision was fulfilled over time.

In 1997, we saw a computer defeat a world chess champion. In 2016, a computer defeated a world master-level player in the Go game. In January 2019, a computer beat top human players 10-1 in the highly complex game StarCraft. Today computer programs are responsible for most stock trading, they act as first defense for online fraud detection, shopping recommendations, and our daily searches. In addition, they power autonomous driving cars, robots, and home devices like Alexa. We are fast approaching Turing's vision.

Today, we honor outstanding computer scientists each year with the Turing award, considered the highest honor in computing. The award is 1 million US dollars.

With his bold imagination, Turing created the computer that powers the modern age. With the same boldness and unflinching optimism, Turing foresaw the era of artificial intelligence and provided a guiding vision.

Unfortunately, Turing did not live to see the exciting developments in this field. He died at home in 1954, either from suicide or accident (there is still dispute). He was only 41 years old.

Turing's torch was passed to four people, who we will meet next.

# 3.

# The Birth of a Field

Santa Monica, California, February 1952

The ocean avenue was with lined palm trees. Herbert Simon took a deep breath, enjoying the spring air. February in Santa Monica is warm and balmy. He thought of the snowy coldness back in Pittsburgh. He turned a corner, and reached a big new building of Rand Corporation.

Herbert Simon was in his mid-30s, tall, energetic, and curious about everything. He was a full professor at Carnegie Institute of Technology (later becoming Carnegie Mellon University). He had moved to Pittsburgh a couple of years before, leaving behind a seven-year career at Illinois Institute of Technology and his department chair position. His book *Administrative Behavior* had gained a significant following. He was a rising star in the field of organizational behavior.

As he entered the Rand building, Simon noticed a buzzing energy. Most people there were in their 20s. Rand in 1952 was a very interesting place. It was a young organization started four years prior, just after the Second World War. It was set up as a think tank for the US military. But it ran like a research lab, organized by groups named "mathematics" and "physics" and so on. Its goal was to encourage intellectual freedom, enabling the researchers to think broadly. Rand hired many academic consultants, the brightest in their fields, including John von Neumann, to help on research. Herbert Simon was one of them.

Simon grew up in Milwaukee, Wisconsin. His father was an electrical engineer who had quite a few patents. This had an influence on Simon, even though he did not choose engineering as his field of study originally. Later in life Simon said, "I have been a closet engineer." Herbert Simon went to University of Chicago and studied in the political science department. He wrote his PhD dissertation in 1943 on administrative behavior, which later turned into a famous book.

At Rand, Simon bumped into a young man named Allen Newell.

"What are you working on?" Simon asked.

"I did some research on game theory, but now I am working on organizational behavior, to see how to apply it to big military groups."

"Really? I am also studying organizational behavior." Simon got excited. He didn't expect to find someone at Rand interested in his topic. He added, "I am most interested in how people make decisions in an organization. For example, I think they do that through trial and error, instead trying to find a perfect solution."

"I remember one of my professors at Stanford talked about such methods. I have always been interested in that." Al beamed with smile.

Simon was deeply intrigued. He learned more about this young man. Allen Newell was barely 25 years old. He joined Rand two years ago, after leaving his PhD program at Princeton. Newell grew up in the San Francisco Bay Area. His father was a radiology professor at Stanford University, very social, and always had a lot of friends coming to visit. Newell attended Stanford University, majoring in physics. He published a research paper when he was a student there. After getting his bachelor's degree, Newell decided to go to Princeton to study mathematics. He took classes from John von Neumann, but discovered he did not like pure mathematics that much. Newell's interests were in applied mathematics and experiments. By the end of the first semester, he made up his mind to strike out on his own. He accepted an offer from Rand.

On his first day at Rand, Newell went to see his supervisor in the mathematics department, J.D. (John Davis) Williams. J.D. looked at him and said, "I have just bought all your time for the year. Here, I give it back to you. Now, go off and do something interesting."

Newell took that freedom and had a blast at Rand. He explored game theory first, then switched to organizational study. That is when he met Herbert Simon. The two of them became instant friends.

"We should keep in touch. Maybe we will find something to work on together," Simon told Newell.

Simon went back to Pittsburgh, but they kept up their conversation. He came back to Rand every summer, and continued lengthy discussions with Newell.

In 1954, Newell got excited about building a computer chess program. He made a presentation at a conference, and went ahead to write a computer program. Simon was excited by the potential of computer too. If a computer can make reasoning about chess moves, why couldn't it reason about mathematical problems?

The next year, Simon suggested that Newell build a program to demonstrate mathematical reasoning. What are the interesting mathematical problems out there? Simon had a copy of *Principia Mathematica* by Alfred Whitehead and Bertrand Russell. They decided to build a program that simulated the reasoning of Bertrand Russell to give mathematical proof. They call this program "Logic Theorist." Its goal was to simulate human reasoning.

As their joint work intensified, Simon convinced Newell to move to Pittsburgh, "you can get a PhD degree and we can work together." For Simon, they were equal partners even though nominally Newell was enrolled as his PhD student.

## Pittsburgh, Pennsylvania, 1955

In the end of 1955, Simon and Newell met daily to complete the Logistic Theorist. This involved coding all the rules into the computer. Without them knowing, they had invented the first AI program, a computer program that reasoned based on symbols.

After the holiday, Simon announced to his class, "Over the holiday, Newell and I designed something that works like a human brain." He could not contain his excitement.

## Dartmouth College, New Hampshire, June 1956

Newell and Simon stood next to the blackboard in a classroom. They were describing their Logic Theorist to the audience. Sitting in the classroom were eight people, all researchers interested in making computers intelligent.

In the audience was a young man, the host of this meeting, John McCarthy. He was the same age of Allen Newell. John McCarthy was an assistant professor at Dartmouth College. He saw the potential of the computer becoming intelligent. Inspired by Turing's 1950 article, McCarthy wanted to bring people together for a one-month summer study. He invited three other people to co-organize this event: Marvin Minsky, his schoolmate at Princeton; Claude Shannon, with whom he co-edited a book on automata a year before, and his former boss at IBM.

McCarthy wrote a funding proposal for this meeting, in which he coined the term "artificial intelligence." He had created the name for a new field.

John McCarthy grew up in Los Angeles in an Irish family. A mathematics genius, McCarthy skipped two years in high school, and entered Caltech at age 17. At Caltech, he skipped the first two years' classes in mathematics since he had already taken them in high school. Influenced by his father, who was a community organizer for workers, McCarthy was a social activist. He became a member of the communist party. In school, his rebel spirit extended to rejection of physical education class. This did not go over well with the university. He was expelled from Caltech.

It was during the Second World War. McCarthy joined the army, and was able to go back to Caltech as a veteran. He finished his remaining undergraduate classes in 1948. Originally, he stayed at Caltech for his graduate study. But he was inspired by a visiting lecture by John von Neumann. McCarthy decided to devote his life to building intelligent machines. He went to Princeton where von Neumann worked, and got his PhD in mathematics in two years.

Another young man in the audience, the same age as McCarthy, was Marvin Minsky. Minsky entered Princeton a year after McCarthy. He received his PhD degree four years later. The two schoolmates formed lifelong friendship that was evident from their work at MIT later.

These four people: John McCarthy, Marvin Minsky, Herbert Simon, and Alan Newell, were later deemed founding fathers of the field artificial intelligence.

A fifth person in this meeting was Claude Shannon. At age 40, he was already a legend at that time. By the time he came to the Dartmouth meeting, he had already invented two fields: One is logic circuit, the foundation of the hardware for modern computers. He invented it at age 21. The other was information theory. He invented it at age 32.

Claude Shannon grew up in a small town in Michigan. He attended University of Michigan at Ann Arbor for his undergraduate study, where he learned about Boole and his logic. In 1936, he went to MIT for graduate study in electric engineering.

One day he worked on the analog computer, and got the following idea: Since True and False can be represented as "1" and "0," the operation on numbers (binary form of 0s and 1s) can be converted to logic operation. For example, when we add two numbers "0" and "1," the result is "1," which is the same as an "OR" operator. Therefore all the mathematical operations such as "add," "multiply," etc. can be done through logic gates, which include "OR," "AND" and later "XOR." The digital circuit was born. Computers built on such circuits are called "digital" computers. While Turing created software architecture for modern computers, Shannon made the hardware possible.

By age 24, Shannon had received his PhD from MIT. He joined the Institute for Advanced Study at Princeton, a prestigious place for researchers. Shannon was very happy that his colleagues included Einstein and John von Neumann.

During the Second World War, Shannon worked at Bell Lab, and worked with Turing for two months when Alan Turing visited Bell Lab.

In 1948, Shannon invented Information theory. The idea is measuring "information" as the number of bits, and the lack of information (uncertainty) by entropy. This work is the foundation of modern communication, and has been applied to many fields such as cryptography, telecommunication, and digital compression such as MP3. Information theory also had big influence on the field of machine learning today.

In 1952, Shannon created a device called "Shannon's mouse," which remembered every step in the maze and found the best path to get through. It achieved what the field of reinforcement learning tried to achieve several decades later.

Unfortunately, Shannon did not work in the field of AI in his later life. He correctly foresaw its difficulty, as it took another 60 years for the field to mature.

In that summer conference in Dartmouth college, Simon and Newell presented the first working AI program, The Logic Theorist. This program used a computer language Simon and Newell invented to process theorem proof. It is a program that demonstrated a computer can "think," which meant at that time reasoning and solving mathematical problems.

Logic Theorist was the only working system at this conference. For others, their work on AI had just started. But the Dartmouth conference brought the major players of this field together, and started artificial intelligence as a field.

***

After the Dartmouth conference, Simon and Newell continued their work and built a strong AI program at

Carnegie Mellon University. Minsky went to MIT, created its AI Lab, and pioneered computer vision. John McCarthy joined Stanford and started Stanford AI Lab. Today, these three universities: Carnegie Mellon, MIT, and Stanford have the top three AI programs in the world.

McCarthy was inspired by the programming of Logic Theorist, and invented his own programming language, LISP, in 1958, which became the major programming language of AI for the next four decades. LISP adopted the linked list and list processing invented by Simon and Newell. In LISP, McCarthy invented objected-oriented programming, which led to the C++ and Java programming languages later.

In 1971, McCarthy received the Turing Award, the highest honor in computing.

# 4.

## Rule-based Systems

At Carnegie Mellon University, Newell and Simon created the new computer science department. Their major focus was rule-based systems.

A rule is described in the form of "If ... Then ..." For example, "If a person grew up in Japan, then this person speaks Japanese."

Human reasoning can be captured by rules. For example, a doctor infers a patient has the flu based on the fever and coughing. A bank detects fraud by applying a rule like, "If a person who sends a large amount of cash three times in a day, this transaction is suspicious." Humans cannot remember all these rules. A computer has the advantage of always remembering them, and always being consistent with them. This gave rise to rule-based systems.

All of the four AI founders (McCarthy and Minsky, in addition to Newell and Simon) worked on rule-based systems. This is natural given their mathematical training.

In 1975, Simon and Newell together received the Turing Award for their "basic contributions to artificial intelligence, the psychology of human cognition, and list processing."

Herbert Simon won the Nobel Prize in economics in 1978 for his work on "decision-making processes within economic organizations." Simon noted that human decisions are bound by time and resources. Our decisions can only be "satisfying," never perfect.

Newell and Simon continued their pursuit in CMU to build such systems for three decades. From 1956 to the late 1990s, expert system research continued to develop, only waning in the late 1990s. If not for the appearance of the Internet and the inundation of large data, expert systems would still be the dominating solution in the AI field.

Rule-based systems have helped many industries, including the US government. Newell's SOAR system, later continued by John Laired at University of Michigan, was adopted by the US military to train their war theatre. It was used in flight simulation.

Simon's student Edward Feigenbaum successfully built an expert system to discover chemical compounds. Later, he built a medical expert system for diagnosis.

At CMU, Simon's other student John McDermott built XCON (eXpert Configurer). It helped Digital Equipment Corporation (DEC) in ordering and configuring its computer systems. Since it used rules for configuration, it was more consistent than those done by humans. It saved the company $40 million per year.

In banking, expert systems were used for fraud detection and loan approval process for a long time.

By the 1980s, expert systems became the poster child of AI. It is the best solution that AI can offer. It's one step forward from pure manual effort, where individual persons make decisions.

But there are some fundamental limitations of expert systems.

First, all the rules are created by humans, or experts. Imagine a medical diagnosis system. We need to ask doctors to put in the rules. A manufacturing processing system, we need ask people who know the process to input the rules. A fraud detection system needs people who are familiar with the fraud to come up with the rules. All of these people are experts in their own domain. The job of the computer is storing these rules and reasoning about them. Therefore, such a system always requires an expert. We have to interview them, and we have to get many experts to agree with each other. What if they have contradictory views? In addition, where do we find so many experts? Human time is expensive. Encoding human knowledge, such as interviews, is time consuming.

The second problem is reasoning on rules. There could be too many rules. There is no quick and definite way to reach our conclusion from a hypothesis. Simon and Newell invented the "heuristic search." In this case, we have to quickly summarize the possible path based on some rule of thumb, or heuristic, which is just a catchier way of saying it. In heuristic, you never know your path is the best, or the second best. You think it is reasonably good, better than the most. But heuristic is not satisfying. There are many cases the experts have not thought of before. There are new situations constantly arising. How do we handle them? Very soon, we see the limitation of expert system in encountering these new situations.

Finally, over time, new rules are added to the system and they may contradict each other. For example, if a rule says "a mammal has four legs," then it will be contradicted by the rule "a bat is a mammal" since a bat has only two legs. In a system with tens of thousands of rules, it is very hard to detect such contradictions. Even after we discover the contradiction, we have to update the old rules. Such updating is very difficult in rule-based systems.

But AI researchers had high hopes for rule-based systems. If only we can encode the right amount of knowledge, if only we can clean up all the contradictions, and if only we can make all the logic reasoning clear, maybe we can capture all the world's knowledge in one AI system? There were two ambitious projects.

One is SOAR, invented by Allen Newell's PhD student John Laird. It tried to mimic human long-term and short-term memory to organize all the rules. The system is thus called a production system. Laird later became a professor at University of Michigan. He brought the system SOAR to Michigan and led his graduate students to develop it further.

When I was a PhD student in Michigan in the late 1990s, John Laird was the head of our AI lab. He sat in a large corner office. I remember passing by his office, admiring his large window view. Laird had the largest research group in our lab, with more than ten students. They gave talks, hosted social barbecues, and ran around our building with their cute experimental devices, including robots. I enjoyed socializing with them.

John was tall and had an imposing physique. I was a little intimated when I saw him. But it turned out he was gentle when spoken to, and he kindly agreed to join my PhD dissertation committee. Even though my work went beyond rule-based systems, John was open minded and supportive.

\*\*\*

The second and most ambitious project of rule-based systems is called Cyc, standing for encyclopedia.

Douglas Lenhat was a Stanford professor. He made a bold proposal: What if we can put all the rules into the system, creating a living encyclopedia that is capable making inference on anything in the world? For his proposal, he was given a large sum of funding.

In 1984, Lenhat moved to Austin, Texas, to start this gigantic project.

Ten years later, Cyc had more than 200 million rules, but was still far from finished. It ran into the difficulty all rule-based systems face: the difficulty of updating rules, checking the consistency of rules, and high cost of adding new rules based on human experts. For example, the computer needs many rules to understand this simple sentence: "Napoleon died on St. Helena. Wellington was greatly saddened." First, it needs to know who is Napoleon and who is Wellington.

Then it needs to know St. Helena is the name of an island. It also needs to know the person who feels saddened has not died yet.

By the time I heard about Cyc in 1996, the project had been around for 12 years, but was nowhere near finishing. This made me deeply disappointed with rule-based systems. Cyc represented our highest hope in rule-based systems, an intelligent system that assimilated all knowledge together. But apparently this approach does not work.

In my view, Cyc failed. Its failure, glaring and public, is also its success. By pushing the limit, it showed the old way does not work, we have to find new solutions to build artificial intelligence.

I was curious then: Is it possible for the machine to learn by itself? How can we make the machine adaptive?

It turned out there was another branch of AI that had been exploring this solution. Their fundamental goal was letting the machine learn by itself, directly from data. This branch of research started at the same time the field of AI started. Its pioneer is Frank Rosenblatt.

# 5.

## Neural Networks: The Beginning

**Buffalo, New York, 1957**

The snow fell hard. Overnight there were more than ten inches on the ground. Frank Rosenblatt watched the whiteness outside the window, lost in his thoughts. He was a tall young man. Just graduated from Cornell University with PhD in psychology, he was enthusiastic about his new work.

For a psychology major, Rosenblatt had an unusual interest in statistics. For him, humans learn not by bullet-proof rules, but by observing chances happening. For example, we believe an apple is sweet after we've tasted it many times.

Here in Buffalo, he joined the university's aeronautical research lab. By now he was 29 years old. Eager to make his mark in the field of science, he worked hard to join the group of people who were at the dawn of creating machine intelligence.

Frank Rosenblatt grew up in a suburb town outside New York City. He went to Bronx High School, where Marvin Minsky also went. This high school has many notable alumni. Today it boasts eight Nobel Prize laureates and many members of the National Academy of Science. Rosenblatt was a year younger than Minsky. They knew of each other, but barely interacted in high school.

While Minsky went off to Harvard University to study mathematics, Rosenblatt went to Cornell University to study psychology. The difference between their academic disciplines is reflected in their approach to the hot problem at that time: How to create artificial intelligence? Mathematicians believed that everything can be resolved by logic, but psychologists take a more experimental approach.

For his research, Rosenblatt did a lot of experiments with animals and people. His work made him deeply interested in how the brain functions, particularly how neurons in the brain process signals and enable people to see, hear, and remember.

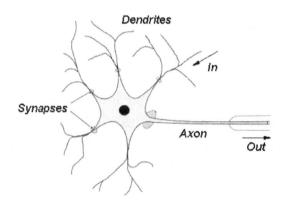

Figure 5.1: An example of a human neuron

He looked at the brain function. Each neuron receives input from its neighboring neurons, and activates and aggregates those signals and then passes the information to the others.

There are 87 billion neurons in our brain that process information. They take light signals and form images in our brain. For example, the image is recognized as a cat, or a dog. The mapping from light signals to a meaningful object is done through some neural function. Rosenblatt calls this "activation function."

What if we can build a computer program that mimics the neurons? He sketched out the design of an artificial neuron on the paper. He called it a "perceptron."

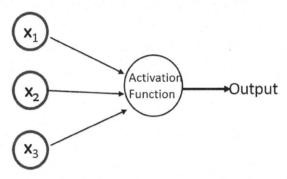

Figure 5.2: An example of a perceptron

A perceptron takes multiple signals and generates an output. The inputs are transformed by an activation function. This activation function can assign different weights to different inputs, sum them up and transform them into a number between 0 and 1. The above figure above shows an example.

This simple yet elegant perceptron concept started the era of the neural network. It is the beginning of machine learning as we know it.

How do we transform the input to a number between 0 and 1? There are some different ways. For example, in the early days, people used a step function. A step function uses a cutoff number. If input is less than this number, then the out is 0, otherwise it is 1. Figure (1) below shows a step function. This function is very simple and easy to interpret. But it is not smooth relative to the value of X. A better function to map inputs to the output is a *Sigmoid Function*, as shown in Figure (2). A sigmoid function is defined as $1/(1+e^{-X})$. Since a sigmoid function is continuous, it is used more often than the step function for neural network. For any y greater than 0.5, we can assign output to be 1. (When x is 0, y is 0.5.)

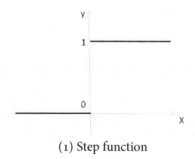

(1) Step function

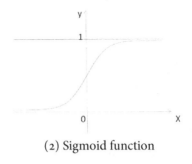

(2) Sigmoid function

Figure 5.3: Two ways of mapping from inputs into the output

How do we apply this neural network to a problem? Let's look at an example.

**Example:** A bank tries to decide whether to approve a loan. A perceptron network is designed to help this decision. The input nodes are information about a customer. We have node 1 (or $x_1$) which represents whether the customer has a savings account, node 2 (or $x_2$) indicates checking account amount, and node 3 (or $x_3$) is the number of months since opening the account. The output y is the action: When y=1, we approve a loan, and when y=0, we reject the loan.

Assume a customer has a savings account, but has negative checking account due to previous borrowing, and this customer's account has been open for the last 5 months, we have $x_1 = 1$ (*Yes*), $x_2 = -3$, $x_3 = 5$. Assume that $W_1 = 0.2$, $W_2 = 0.6$, $W_1 = 0.3$. Then, y=sigmoid ($W_1 x_1 + W_2 x_2 + W_3 x_3$)=sigmoid (-0.1). We have y=0.48. Since it is less than 0.5, the output will be 0, meaning we will not approve the loan.

As you can see, the concept of the neural network is very general. It can apply to any kind of problem. Our decision, or perception, is a function of what we know (or see). For example, when we say a picture shows a cat, that's because we see the lines and shapes in the picture. These lines and shapes can be converted into numbers. In fact, everything on a picture can be converted into numbers. Each picture is composed of pixels, or a group of numbers. Here is an example of picture of the number "7":

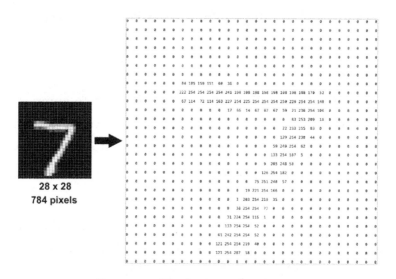

**28 x 28**
**784 pixels**

Figure 5.4: Pixel values of an image

Human sees the left picture, but the computer sees the right one, with all the numbers. Each of these numbers can be corresponding to an input neuron.

Rosenblatt tried to build perceptron into a hardware, which directly takes input and gives an output.

Rosenblatt's perceptron generated a lot of enthusiasm and public interest. Interviewed by the *New York Times*, Rosenblatt made the following prediction: The perceptron is going to be "the embryo of an electronic computer that will be able to walk, talk, see, write, reproduce itself, and be conscious of its existence." Such a prediction was bold for the times. Almost all of his predictions became true 60 years later, except "conscious of its existence."

In 1962, He published the book *Principles of Neurodynamics: Perceptrons and the Theory of Brain Mechanisms*. This book postulated the concept of the perceptron, and generated excitement.

How do we train this network based on the data we see? The weights are not determined by humans. Instead they are learned from data.

Minsky was not happy with the attention Rosenblatt got. He was not convinced the perceptron could work. At the conference where they met, Minsky and Rosenblatt had heated arguments.

In 1969, Minky published a book, stealing the title from his opponent, *Perceptron*. What can be better than using your opponent's invention and ridiculing it? Better at mathematics, and more eloquent in writing, Minsky attacked the perceptron by oversimplifying it as single-layer neural network. A single-layer neural network has one input layer directly going into output, thus lacking internal layers (or *hidden layers*).

In fact, Rosenblatt already had hidden layers in his original design. His multi-layer design was actually cited years later (in 1995) by Vapnik when he proposed support-vector machines, a popular machine learning method.

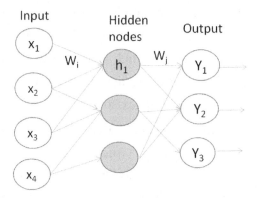

Figure 5.5: A 2-layer neural network (with 1 hidden layer)

A multi-layer neural network has at least one hidden layer. Adding one hidden layer allows the input to transform one more time. With two hidden layers, we can transform the input twice. This means we can derive complex functions on the input. If we can add three or more layers, we can model more complex situations in the world. This is the idea of "deep learning." Today, deep learning has become almost a synonym of AI. The power of deep learning goes all the way back to Rosenblatt's invention, the perceptron that models human neurons.

Rosenblatt was deeply hurt by Minsky's book. He was misrepresented and publicly ridiculed. Adding insult to injury, the research on his perceptron was not going well. Rosenblatt invented a forward propagation method, this did not work well to train the network.

The research funding for Rosenblatt's group suddenly stopped. Rosenblatt stopped his work on neural network and turned his attention to brain research.

On his birthday in 1971, Rosenblatt went sailing in Chesapeake Bay. He was happy being away from the taxing research. The boat capsized. He died at age 43.

But his legacy was redeemed today. He influenced Nils Nilsson to join SRI to "build a brain." Nilsson has become influential in the AI field. He inspired Vladimir Vapnik and other machine learning researchers.

In 2004, almost 50 years after the invention of perceptron, the Institute of Electrical and Electronics Engineers (IEEE) established Frank Rosenblatt Award. Among the recipients are Vladimir Vapnik (in 2012) and Geoffrey Hinton (in 2014), who you will soon meet in the next chapter.

Minsky's book had a devastating effect on the research on neural network. Mainstream AI researchers didn't touch this subject. Funding dried up in this field in the 1970s.

During this time, some researchers outside the mainstream still pushed forward the development of neural networks. One of them was Geoffrey Hinton.

# 6.

## The Revival of Neural Networks

**San Diego, CA, 1979**

He had always been an outsider, but he didn't care. Geoff Hinton walked through the UC San Diego campus, thinking of the upcoming meeting with his friends James McClean and David Rumelhart. At the psychology department, they formed a group to study neural networks, but the rest of AI community was not that much interested.

Growing up in England, Hinton attended King's College at Cambridge University, where Alan Turing used to study and work. Hinton chose experimental psychology as his undergraduate major, the same subject that Frank Rosenblatt focused on. He was fascinated by human brains and particularly how to create intelligence based on that principle.

When he decided on what to study for his PhD program, he heard about the program at University of Edinburgh on machine intelligence. Hinton moved to Edinburgh with no hesitation. He received his PhD in AI there in 1977.

Even with a PhD under his belt, it was hard to find a job. Neutral network was not a popular subject then. After a short stint in England, Hinton came to University of California at San Diego as a post-doctor fellow in 1979. He was convinced that an artificial neural network was the way to build AI, even though the mainstream AI looked down at this "low-level" approach. This is the time when rule-based system was at its height, logic reasoning was the dominating topic.

At UC San Diego, Hinton found kindred spirits. At the department of psychology, he met James McClelland and David Rumelhart. They were all believers in neural networks. They felt this was the best path to achieve true intelligence.

It's interesting to see that all the pioneers of neural networks came from the psychology department.

"Why don't we start a project to show people that neural networks can do many things?" They started to meet twice a week and work intensively. They thought this project could be done in six months. In reality, it took them five years.

They attracted other people to join their effort. They called themselves connectionists, and coined the name PDP (Parallel Distributed Processing) group for their group. One of the participants was Michael Jordan, who later became a professor at UC Berkeley. Jordan influenced his PhD student Andrew, who has become a leading figure in the deep learning (using deep neural networks) revolution.

During this time (in 1982), Geoff got a faculty job at CMU. He moved to Pittsburgh, but continued his research. The rest of the group continued to meet weekly in UC SD.

By the time they finished the project in 1986, they put all the findings in a two volume book called *Parallel Distributed Processing*. (It seems neural network was not a fashionable term then, which explains the choice of words.)

The PDP group achieved two major breakthroughs that revived the neural network field. Both inventions had Geoff Hinton's input. The first breakthrough was proving both theoretically and experimentally that multi-layer neural networks can represent any function, and thus work on any type of learning task: images, language, etc. Minsky's criticism on neural network centered around a single-layer neural network, and he mistakenly believed that the same problem would hold for a multi-layer neural network.

How do we apply a multi-layer neural network to do image recognition? Let's take a look at this simple problem: We would like to classify images into certain head poses: left, center, and right.

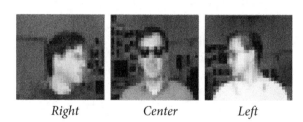

*Right*      *Center*      *Left*

We first segment a photo into small regions. For simplicity, we divide the image into 4 by 4 segments or 16 regions. Each of these regions will correspond to one input node. Thus we have a total of 16 input nodes. The value of each input node is the grey scale of that region.

We have three output nodes, each representing a head pose, "left," "center," and "right." The value for each output node is a number between 0 and 1. We use one layer of hidden nodes.

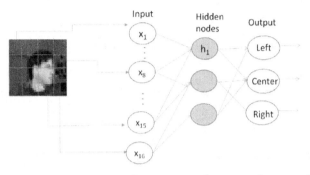

Figure 6.1: Head pose detection with a neural network

We are going to train our neural network on many examples of face photos. Each training photo is labeled with one of the three poses. In addition, each photo is divided into 16 regions and the grey scale of each region is extracted.

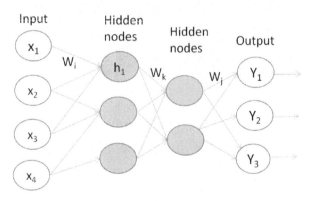

Figure 6.2: A three-layer neural network

The second invention is *backpropagation.* It fundamentally changed how a neural network can be trained. It updates the weights of a neural network backwards. For every data instance, we calculate the error as the difference between predicted output and the actual output. This error is used to update the weight between the last hidden layer and the output layer. Then it propagates back to the previous layer.

Exactly how much weight do we adjust? Image the error space is like mountains and valleys. Our goal is to reach the bottom (smallest error). Which path should we take to reach to the bottom faster? The path with steepest slope is the fastest one. Mathematically we can find the steepest slope on a surface by drawing a tangent line. This slope is called the "gradient" of the standing point. Therefore the weight updating in neural networks uses "gradient descent." Hinton applied gradient descent to weight updating, starting from the last layer, and all the way to the previous layers. Each weight is updated by its gradient on the error space.

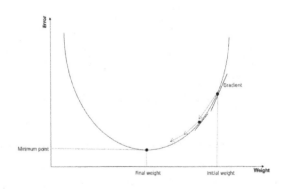

Figure 6.3: Illustration of Gradient Descent

Backpropagation has gradient descent as its core method and formulated a systematic way of updating a neural network. It made learning a neural network efficient and stable.

Backpropagation has become the dominating method of learning neural networks, and it revived the field of neural networks.

Another contribution of Hinton was inventing autoencoder. By its name, auto means it learns about itself. The autoencoder is a multi-layer neural network, where the input is the same as output. For example: a cat picture is fed into the neural network. The output of this neural network is still the cat.

Hinton accepted a faculty position at University of Toronto in 1987. The largest city in Canada, Toronto resembles London more than any American cities he lived in. Hinton has stayed in Toronto ever since, except a one-time stint back in London for creating a neuroscience department at University College London.

By the mid-1990s, neural networking had been applied to many domains, such as credit scoring, fraud detection, computer vision, computer speech, and robotics. The most successful application was postal office letter scanning that recognized handwritten addressees automatically.

In 1992, Hinton wrote an article for *Scientific America*, explaining the details of neural networks and the basic training algorithms. For the general public, neural networks were interesting again.

Neural network has had a rebirth. Even though it is slow, it has come back to life.

# 7.

## The Rise of Machine Learning

In the mid-1980s, another machine learning method was invented. It became a strong contender to neural networks. This method has ties to rule-based systems. It automatically summarizes rules in a tree-like format. It is called the decision tree. Its inventor is Ross Quinlan.

Ross Quinlan grew up in Australia. He got his bachelor's degree from University of Sidney, then pursued his PhD in computer science in the United States. He was the first person who received a PhD degree from the Department of Computer Science at the University of Washington in 1968. After that, he went back to University of Sidney to teach. Quinlan enjoyed programming, even after he became a professor.

In 1978, he visited Stanford University where he came up with the idea of summarizing rules in a tree format. He was sitting in a lecture and was intrigued by the challenge posed by the professor: how to learn the rules to predict the result of a chess game. He created the first decision tree algorithm, which can summarize rules very quickly, from 29,000 training cases. This algorithm can be used for chess prediction, but also for many other tasks such as spam detection, user click predictions, and bank loan decisions.

In 1986, Ross Quinlan published his paper "Induction of Decision Trees" in *Machine Learning* Journal. The decision tree algorithm has since been known by a wide public and embraced by the AI researchers. It quickly rose to prominence in the 1990s, and became the dominating machine learning algorithm for the next two decades.

PayPal in its early days, still a startup, used decision tree for fraud detection and it helped create a viable business. Google used decision tree for its initial search ranking. Yahoo! used decision tree for its spam filters. Banks used decision trees for loan decisions.

How does decision tree work? Let's look at the following example:

A customer comes into the bank, wanting to apply for a loan. The bank loan officer looks at this customer's history with the bank, and needs to make a decision. Should he approve the loan or not?

In the old days (before the computer age), the decision was made by the human judgment of the loan officer. He used his own experience and some information such as: Does he look trustable? Is he currently deposit sufficient? How is his income? As you can see, these are just rules of thumb that change from one bank representative to another.

After the 1970s, rule-based systems (expert systems) were adopted by banks. The bank officer would use a computer program, which suggests a decision based on the rules such as, "IF this person has less than $5,000 in savings and he has never applied for a loan before, THEN do not approve." Such rules are created from interviewing with experienced bank loan officers (experts) and coded into a computer program. It automated the loan decision process. But the system is rigid. It requires many experienced officers, and the rules do not change over time.

Consider the decision tree approach. It first looks at the historical data, where some loans were repaid, and some were not. Based on the data, a decision tree gives the bank the following suggestion:

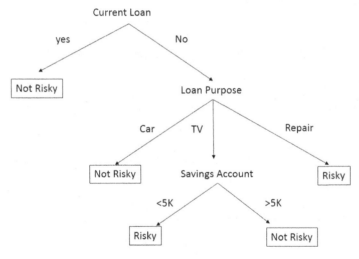

Figure 7.1: A decision tree for bank loan

This tree is automatically derived from all the loan data. The data would include the basic attributes of a loan that show up in this tree: duration of the loan, the borrower's savings, whether the borrower currently has loan with bank, and the purpose of the loan. The data also contains outcomes of each loan.

Below is an example.

| Loan ID | Duration (years) | Savings ($k) | Current Loans | Loan Purpose | Credit Risk |
|---------|------------------|--------------|---------------|--------------|-------------|
| 1 | 1 | 10 | Yes | TV | No |
| 2 | 2 | 4 | No | TV | Yes |
| 3 | 5 | 75 | No | Car | No |
| 4 | 10 | 66 | No | Repair | Yes |
| 5 | 5 | 83 | Yes | Car | No |
| 6 | 1 | 11 | No | TV | No |
| 7 | 4 | 99 | Yes | Car | No |

*Table: An example of a bank loan outcomes*

The loan officer can use the decision tree above, plug in a new customer's data, and quickly use decide whether the loan is risky or not.

Note that there are no more human experts required. The computer can summarize data from hundreds of thousands of loans, which gives the computer more a comprehensive view than a single expert knows in his lifetime. In addition, the system can update the tree as soon as there is new loan data, thus it is adaptive.

Decision trees demonstrated the power of automatically extracting rules, or machine learning. The goal of machine learning is summarizing pattern from the data, and making a prediction on a new instance.

How is a decision tree constructed from data? Without going into all the details, in short, Quinlan selects a root node and its branching nodes based on "entropy," a concept from Claude Shannon's information theory. The entropy measures how much information each node carries.

Both neural networks and decision trees were widely used in the 1990s and early 2000s, with decision trees used more often as they are faster and easier to interpret. Both methods required training data. The training contains examples with their corresponding outcomes. This is called supervised learning, as the machine needs to know previous examples to predict similar cases in the future. The prediction is typically binary, "yes" or "no." Therefore, they are called binary classifications.

It turned out many problems can be reduced to a binary outcome. If you want to send out marketing mail to a group of residents, choosing whom to send to is equivalent to finding out who would or would not respond to your campaign.

Displaying search results to the users is discovering what documents would have higher chance of click through. It is a binary outcome of a link will be clicked or not. Customer churn prediction is equivalent to classifying a customer into a churn group or "not churn" group.

In 2008, Obama's campaign looked at donors' profiles (people who donate vs people who do not donate), and created fund raising strategies. In this campaign, they looked at people who were top donors, and derived that these were single women in their 40s or older. The fundraising campaign attended by George Clooney was a big success.

Through binary classification we can convert many problems into a working machine learning problem.

Since binary classification is powerful, another algorithm was invented for this purpose, and became very popular in the early 2000s, surpassing decision trees in many applications. Its inventor was Vladimir Vapnik.

Vapnik was part of the exodus of top-level scientists from Russia after the fall of the Soviet Union. Vapnik was the head of the computer science department of the Institute of Control Sciences in Moscow when he left in 1990. He was already 54 years old. He got his PhD in statistics and had been with the same institute for 26 years.

Vapnik started his new life in the United States working in the Bell Lab. Yet, he continued to devote himself to research, as if age never defined him.

In 1995, at age 59, Vapnik published his landmark paper, "Support-Vector Networks." In this paper, he first reviewed Frank Rosenblatt's perceptron, and turned to his attention to the binary classification problem.

In order to separate two classes efficiently, we can construct a linear hyperplane coming between these two classes and separating them cleanly. To construct this straight line, you only need a few points that are closest, which are called support vectors. The method that automatically generate this separating line is called a Support-Vector Machine (SVM).

An SVM separates the data into two regions with a hyperplane. The goal is to find the separating hyperplane that generates the widest margin between the two classes.

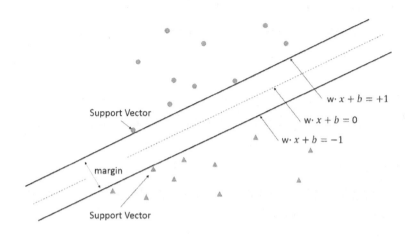

Figure 7.2: Linear SVM: Linearly Separable Data Set

Wider margins result in smaller generalization errors. If the margin about the decision boundary is large, slight perturbations in the data do not impact the model. In the figure above, the data points are divided into two classes: triangles and dots. The separating hyperplane is illustrated as the dashed line in the above figure. Notice that it correctly separates the two classes. The bolder lines indicate the margin. Notice that no data points are within the margin of the separating hyperplane. There are many possible separations for this data set. In fact either of the bold lines could be a separator, however the separator with the largest margin will generalize best.

The learning process searches for the "support vectors" that consist of data points that uniquely define the hyperplane and yield the maximum margin between positive support vectors (above the hyperplane) and negative support vectors (below the hyperplane).

When there are a huge number of observations in comparison to the number of features, SVM can employ a kernel technique. The kernel technique will produce a curved boundary between the two classes. This boundary will still have the property that the margin will be maximized. For linear SVM the kernel is simply linear. However for more complicated kernels, there is a parameter, gamma, which indicates the complexity of the kernel. The best value for gamma is once again found through cross validation.

The kernel technique pushes the data into a higher dimension, in which case the points can be linearly separable with a hyperplane. One common example of moving data between dimensions is that of making maps of Earth. Earth is a sphere, yet it can be represented as a flat surface on a paper map. A two dimensional map is depicted on the left side of the below figure. When the plane cuts through the sphere slightly below the equator the boundary created on the map is a circle. On the two dimensional map, the data is not linearly separable, however in three dimensions the data is linearly separable.

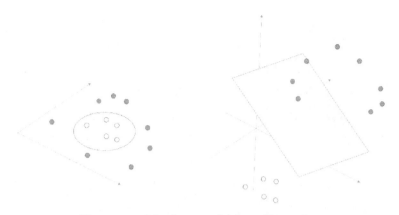

Figure 7.3: Moving to a higher dimension

In conclusion, SVM classifiers maximize the margin of the decision boundary between the two classes. SVM classifiers require numerical data as input. They work very well in higher dimensions. They work well with sparse data. They are not affected by outliers.

SVM simplifies machine learning by finding support vectors without computing on all points. This makes learning much faster.

SVM quickly became a major machine learning method in the first decade of 21st century. Owing to open-source packages, many companies adopted SVM as their main machine learning method. It is more accurate and faster. However, projecting into higher dimensions comes with computational cost. A lot of research in the 2000s and early 2010s was studying how to avoid using higher dimensions, by simply using more data. It's shown more data leads to better results, even the model is simple. Linear SVM became the main method used by large companies.

So far introduced were three machine learning methods commonly used by data scientists: decision tree, neural network, and support-vector machine. For most datasets, there is no definite answer on which method is better. In practice, researchers run all three methods through the training dataset, and pick one method that gives them the best performance. The training by all three methods is reasonably fast (most times neural network is the slowest).

The Internet Age brings big data, which is too large for humans to process or inspect every hour or even minute. It calls for automatic data processing. In addition, we want to process data intelligently. This makes machine learning an attractive tool. Big data drives the development of machine learning. The landscape of machine learning is forever changed.

# 8.

## Chatterbots

In 1966, Joseph Weizenbaum, a researcher at the MIT AI lab, wrote a computer program that makes conversation with a user. If a user types in something, it replies back. He named this program Eliza. Here is a transcript of a dialog:

User: My boyfriend made me come here.

Eliza: Your boyfriend made you come here?

Use: He says I'm depressed much of the time.

Eliza: I am sorry to hear you are depressed.

Use: It is true, I am unhappy.

Eliza: Do you think coming here will help you not to be unhappy?

Use: I need some help, that much seems certain.

Eliza: What would it mean to you if you got some help?

User: Perhaps I could learn to get along with my mother.

Eliza: Tell me more about your family.

It is little wonder that people got fascinated with Eliza. Some people had long conversations with Eliza and poured out their hearts. It was as if they were talking to a real person. Weizenbaum was shocked when his secretary asked him to leave the room when she was having a conversation with Eliza. This alarmed Weizenbaum and so he tried to show that there is no AI behind Eliza.

Joseph Weizenbaum came to the United States with his parents from Nazi Germany in 1936. His family avoided the tragic fate of Jews left behind: being sent to concentration camps. Weizenbaum joined the US Army, working as a meteorologist in the Second World War. After the war, he returned to university to get his master's degree in mathematics. He was among the first few people who built digital computers. In 1964, he joined the MIT AI lab as a researcher.

Weizenbaum was surprised by the strong response to Eliza. Almost 30 years later, I had that same response when I got to know Eliza for the first time.

I was sitting in a large classroom in the Electric Engineering and Computer Science (EECS) building at University of Michigan. It was my first AI class. There were about 200 other students around me. On the podium stood a young professor, dark haired, wearing a crisp white shirt, confident and energetic. After he showed a transcript from Eliza, the whole class was wowed. I was deeply mesmerized.

But the professor, Michael Wellman, quickly dispelled our illusion: "There is nothing magical about this program. All it did was pattern matching." What is pattern matching? I was all ears. Wellman explained a sequence of words can form a "pattern." For example:

"I feel *" is a pattern, where the "*" can be replaced by any word. This pattern would match anything sentence such as: "I feel happy.", "I feel angry.", or "I feel bad."

Pattern matching is detecting such patterns in the string. In the early days of computing, it took some programming skill to write a pattern matching program to change words from "you" to "I" and so on. Eliza used this simple method, creating dialogs that looked human.

With such simple pattern matching and word swap, Eliza behaved as if she understood you. What if we could put more pattern in them?

Eliza inspired many people. A few systems have been created to imitate Eliza, but they do not do well. If you talk to those systems, you will quickly realize they are just a computer program which has no understanding of you.

***

Hugh Loebner has always been fascinated by AI. After he received his PhD in demography from University of Massachusetts - Amherst, he made a fortune in his business. Intrigued by Eliza, and inspired by Turing's vision, he wondered if he could set up a contest that encouraged AI researchers to move toward passing the Turing test.

In 1990, Loebner created a prize for any programmer whose AI could pass a Turing test, meaning that they could fool you into thinking that the AI was a human. This prize generated a lot of interest. From 1990 to today, this is held every year.

It was Loebner's intent to offer $100,000 dollars and a solid gold medal to anyone who can pass the Turing test. It spurred many chatterbots, some very interesting.

Some people question this method of testing intelligence. After all, we can have a trivial program that mimics human talking, and tricks you into believing that it is a human. For example, the Shakespeare program, which knows deeply about Shakespeare (excerpts from Loebner contest):

Judge: What is your favorite Shakespearian play?

Computer: King Lear, I also like many of the comedies. How about you?

Judge: Sonnets, also the comedies but the tragedies are my favorites. Are you familiar with Hamlet?

Computer: The college kid who came home and found his mom had married the guy who murdered his dad just a little month before. You might say so.

Unfortunately, all the programs submitted to this test are using phrase patterns and try to use a large list of responses to accomplish the task. Anticipating patterns has its limitation as the program designer has only limited arsenal of words that they can think out of his head. (Today, we use statistical approach, which summarizes many users' patterns.) As interesting as it is, when a user asks in a different way, the program breaks down.

One of the notable participants was Alice, which stands for Artificial Linguistic Internet Computer Entity. The founder of ALICE was Richard Wallace. He got his PhD in computer science from CMU. He started building Alice in 1995.

Alice won the Loebner prize in 2000, 2001, and 2004 and has been on the Internet for a long time. It is more sophisticated than Eliza, and it has more knowledge.

Alice is available online. You can chat with Alice in your browser.

Alice also started one of the earliest open-source collaborations. More than 500 developers contributed to the code.

The academic AI community moved away from the Loebner prize. They felt that AI was far away from making meaningful conversation. They thought the Loebner contest might lead people to create more pattern matching programs instead solving real AI problems. But the development of chatterbots has generated public interest for studying AI. In fact, the movie *Her* was inspired by Eliza instead of the academic AI research.

I myself, a conventional AI researcher, followed the Loebner prize with deep interest, and always wondered if I could create a real AI to win that prize.

While chatterbots do not contribute to the main AI fields, they are useful in personal assistants. That's because they offer a way to form quick responses to some random questions from the users.

In late 1990s there was a surge of chatterbots, partly because of the rise the Internet and people starting to feel it was possible to provide this service to others. Startups sprung up, using chatterbots to provide customer support, training for employees, and for mood lifting.

All the home assistants, or conversational bots, need to have a chatterbot component. From Siri to Microsoft Cortana to Alexa, chatterbots have been indispensable in interacting with users. It gives a sharp and quick reply without worrying deeply what the user means.

It is very apparent that Alexa uses chatterbot strategy

User: "Alexa, where were you born?"

Alexa: "I was born in Seattle."

User: "Alexa, you are stupid."

Alexa: "That's not nice to say."

Similarly Siri also adopted chatterbot as part of her answering strategy.

User: "What is zero divided by zero?"

Siri: "Imagine that you have zero cookies and you split them evenly among zero friends. How many cookies does each person get? See? It doesn't make sense. And Cookie Monster is sad that there are no cookies, and you are sad that you have no friends."

Siri says you have no friends. Does she understand what you said? Of course not.

Is it possible to build a personal assistant that totally discards chatterbot and goes into deep meaningful conversation? This is equivalent to asking: How far can we push machines in understanding human languages? Since the beginning of AI, this has been our dream: to build a machine that understands us. We want to a create a program like "her" who can truly understand us and help us. How well are we doing today? Today's chatterbot, those we see popping up on bank websites or online stores, are much more sophisticated.

# 9.

## Speech Recognition: The Road to Siri and Alexa

Pittsburgh, Pennsylvania, 1974

James Baker was dismayed by the results. He poured over the program again but could not find anything wrong. He sat in the lab contemplating what to do.

It was 1974, he was working on his PhD degree at Carnegie Mellon University, wanting to build a computer program that could listen and recognize continuous speech with 1,000 words. When his advisor Raj Reddy gave him that task, he was excited. But the results now made it seem impossible.

Speech recognition was moving slowly then. It started in 1952 when IBM demonstrated the first speech recognition system for recognizing digits of 0–9 uttered by a single speaker. The speaker had to pause between words. For 20 years, the progress was slow. In 1971, Allen Newell put a proposal to DARPA (Defense Advanced Research Project Agency). He proposed that they could build a system that understood continuous speech of a vocabulary of 1,000 words in 5 years. This was a big leap over the previous systems. For this reason, Newell hired Reddy away from Stanford University. Reddy got to work. He convinced James Baker to join his PhD program at CMU.

James Baker got interested in speech recognition when he met a beautiful young woman named Janet at graduate school. Janet studied animal vocalization. Later she switched to studying human speech. Being in love, James was intrigued by everything Janet did. He looked at Janet's digital recording of human speech and could see some obvious patterns. With his mathematical training, Baker thought he could extract the patterns and map them to human words.

Baker stumbled into the field of speech recognition. Human speeches are sound waves in the air, which can be captured by a device and transformed into data, as shown in the below figure.

Figure 9.1: An example of audio data

First, we divide the sound signal into short segments. Typically, the segments are between 20 milliseconds (ms) and 30 milliseconds and they are overlapped by 10 ms. This is called short-time analysis. Each segment can be transformed into a feature vector. Each feature vector can be mapped to a possible phoneme. Phonemes are basic linguistic units such as /K/, /AE/ or /T/. There are about 44 phonemes in English.

The steps of speech recognition are shown in the figure below:

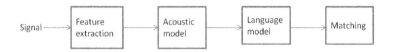

Figure 9.2: Steps of speech recognition

An acoustic model describes possible sequences of phonemes for a given word. Once we have a sequence of phonemes like, /AY/, /L/, /AY/, and /K/, we will convert them to a sequence of words. Researchers have built a large pronunciation dictionary, where we can look for the words based on phonemes:

EYE - /AY/

I - /AY/

LIKE - /L/ /AY/ /K/

CANDY - /K/ /AE/ /N/ /D/ /IY/

For the above example, the words could be "I like" or "eye like." Which is more possible?

A language model which tells us how likely a word is to be followed by another word. "Like" is more likely to follow "I" than "eye." Other examples are: "A good man" is more likely than "a good map," and "I am mad" is more likely than "I am mat."

James Baker realized that a word is mostly related to the word before, but not closely related to two words before. In other words, the probability of the word "candy" happening after "like" has little to the word before "like" (that is "I"). This property is called the Markov process. (Markov is a Russian mathematician who invented the concept of this process in 1913. He demonstrated this by counting the patterns of word sequences in poems.)

In general, the Markov process simplifies the relationship in a sequence of events. Each event depends only on its previous event, but not two events before. This simplifies computation greatly.

Speech recognition is looking at two Markov processes happening at the same time. One is the sequence of phonemes uttered by the speaker, another Markov process is the sequence of words intended by the speaker. The word sequence is hidden behind the phoneme sequence. One process (for phonemes) is observed, and one is hidden. The model that describes such two Markov processes is called the Hidden Markov Model (HMM). This gives us an integrated model for speech process.

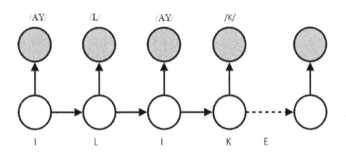

Figure 9.3: Hidden Markov Model for Speech Recognition

HMM introduces statistics into speech recognition research. It is in contrast with a rule-based approach as it introduces more "knowledge," which Allen Newell believed a speech system needed. Baker realized that statistics were more powerful in describing the relationship or generating the phenomenon we see. Thus, Baker introduced, for the first time, the concept of randomness (stochastic process) into the speech recognition research. This opened the door to using machine learning in this field later.

HMM became the foundation of speech recognition for the next three decades. It also became the foundation for other natural language processing tasks, such as tagging, and named entity detection (identifying a person's name, a song name, or a location name).

HMM was very successful and powerful. It enabled Baker to achieve the accuracy for continuous speech with 1,000 words for the first time.

Jim Baker graduated in 1975, the year CMU successfully completed the DARPA challenge. Baker's work at CMU was continued by other PhD students of Raj Reddy. One of them was Xuedong Huang, who built the Sphinx-II system that was open-sourced later and helped many speech recognition researchers.

After graduation, Baker worked in a small company for a few years before he decided to create his own company. He and his wife, Janet, started the company Dragon Systems in 1982. Baker's ambition at that time was putting speech recognition systems on desktops where people could use them at home. This was very ambitious due to two reasons: The computing power was not yet big enough, personal computers had very limited on-board memory then; and the language processing model was not there. But Jim Baker realized that computer power would eventually grow, and Dragon Systems could roll out the system in a different phase. He was deeply passionate about making this technology a practical solution. The company put in a lot of R&D money.

At that time, IBM, had its eye on the market for speech technology, and they had a very large team and corporate funding. Dragon Systems was a tiny company with no venture funding. For the next 15 years, these two companies competed in the speech software market. Through Baker's hard work and dedication, Dragon Systems triumphed. In a consumer evaluation of speech systems, Dragon Systems won 90% of evaluation items. This is a David vs. Goliath story.

In 1997, Dragon Systems was acquired by Nuance (the later name of the parent company). After the acquisition, Dragon Systems' flagship product – Dragon Naturally Speaking, continue to flourish in the speech market.

Dragon Naturally Speaking was the first commercial software that allowed people to dictate speech, which inspired many researchers in the speech domain. Years later (in 2007), I was happy to have a copy of the software, which was still popular then.

## Stockholm, Sweden, 1997

Nikko Ström was finishing his PhD program at The Royal Institute of Technology (KTH). He presented his PhD dissertation titled "Automatic Continuous Speech Recognition with Rapid Speaker Adaptation for Human/Machine Interaction." It incorporated two groundbreaking papers he wrote during his PhD years.

The first paper was published in 1992, which combined time-delay neural networks with a recurrent neural network (RNN) for speech recognition. A recurrent neural network is defined relative to a feedforward neural network. In a feedforward neural network, information flows in one direction from the input to the output. In a recurrent neural network, information can flow backwards, from output back to the input, or from the hidden layer back to the same hidden layer or to previous layer. Thus, the network is like having a loop. See the figure below.

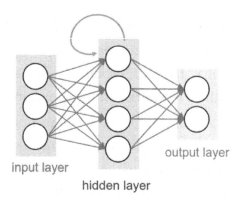

Figure 9.4: Recurrent Neural Network

A recurrent neural network captures the influence of previous input. Thus, it is suitable for modeling sequential information, such as speech or text.

With RNN, we can model a Hidden Markov Model easily. In fact, RNN performs so much better than any traditional speech model that speech researchers started to adopt it in their work.

In another paper published in 1996, Ström introduced a method for speaker adaptation, which can also be used to identify a speaker.

During his PhD years, Ström also wrote an open-source neural network software called NICO (Neural Inference Computation), a toolkit which has been downloaded thousands of times, mostly by researchers in the field of speech recognition. Designed for speech, NICO ended up being a general purpose toolkit for building artificial neural networks and training with the backpropagation learning algorithms. (While it is no longer a state-of-the-art toolkit in 2019, Ström still recommends it as a good choice for fast training and evaluation on large networks.)

The practical aspect of Ström's PhD research was that he had created, according to himself, "the world's first continuous speech recognizer for the Swedish language."

After graduation Ström joined MIT's Spoken Language Systems Group as a postdoctoral researcher. He was a leading contributor to the Galaxy-II architecture, which had a centralized hub mediating the interaction among a suite of language servers. It was designated as the first reference architecture for the new DARPA Communicator Program.

In 2000, Ström left MIT to join the voice tech startup Tellme Networks in California as a speech engineer.

## Mountain View, California, 2000

Tellme was started in 1999. From 1999 to 2000, Tellme raised $238 million. Eric Jackson, a tech and media investor, commented that, in many ways, Tellme "were the first unicorn. Raising hundreds of millions of dollars in the late 90s dot-com bubble from Kleiner Perkins, Jim Barksdale and many others on the promise of delivering 'dial tone 2.0.' For the first time, you'd be able to pick up the phone and use your voice to ask for anything you wanted."

Tellme specialized in telephone-based applications. It pioneered the idea of voice portals, a web-style search via telephones. Telephones could recognize users' voice commands and respond with appropriate content. The company established an information number which provided news announcements, weather forecasts, sports summaries, business searches, stock market quotations, driving directions, and similar amenities. This call-in service was announced in 2000 and received a high usage. The company also received a lot of feedback. By 2006, Tellme's phone network processed more than 2 billion unique calls.

Tellme also provided third-party technical support and hosting services for some big companies to automate their customer service.

Nikko Ström threw himself into the hard work of building the voice technology. His hard work was recognized. In 2006, he was promoted to director of speech technology.

In March 2007, Microsoft acquired Tellme for $800 million. Tellme had built up an incredible team of young talent by the late 1990s. Many team members have now become prominent figures in Silicon Valley. For example, Ellen Pao became CEO of Reddit, John Gianandrea became the head of Google AI and recently joined Apple, and Alfred Lin became a partner at Sequoia Capital, one of the largest venture capital firms.

After the acquisition, Ström moved to Seattle to work in the Core Speech Recognition Team at Microsoft, where he helped to commercialize speech recognition for Microsoft.

In April 2007, Google rolled out "Google 4-1-1," which enabled people to call from any phone to ask 411. With Google's wide consumer reach, this service generated a lot of user interest, and a lot of speech data were collected. This helped to improve Google's speech recognition system.

*** 

During that time I was working in Bosch Research's natural language group. We were building a speech dialog system for cars.

At the time, we were frustrated with the speech recognition accuracy as it just would not go down. We suffered from the following problems:

1. Lack of speech data: User data in cars were not collected

2. There is not enough computing power in cars to process the speech

We hired someone to enter speech grammar for the system, and we collected all possible nouns (using a dictionary) that could be spoken by a user. This included 3 million business names and 1,300 cities in California. Our job was recognizing them quickly so that we could handle user commands in the car: "Take me to John Doe clinic in Walnut Creek." In this simple command, there is a business name and a city name to be recognized.

After seeing Google's success in collecting speech data and cloud processing, I realized speech recognition systems have to be server based, or hosted in the cloud. This allows for hosting large amounts of data for speech model training. The trained model can be sent back to the local system (client). This is, in fact, the model of all speech-based systems today. All computing is done in the cloud. Your home robot or speaker has a body in your room, but its brain lives somewhere far away on a remote server.

## Menlo Park, California, 2007

In the same year Tellme was acquired, another company started in Silicon Valley. Its name was Siri.

Siri was founded by a group of researchers at SRI, located a few streets away from the campus of Stanford University. SRI was originally part of Stanford, but had since become independent. Their research was mostly funded by the US government for general research. SRI had a large AI group which pioneered robots and speech research.

Adam Cheyer was a research engineer at SRI's speech group. He wanted to take it to the next level. He discussed this with Dag Kittlaus, an entrepreneur in residence at SRI, and Tom Gruber who worked on ontology. The three of them decided to co-found Siri in late 2007. They raised $8.5 million by early 2018.

Siri's founding was prompted by the release of the first iPhone in June 2007. The iPhone fundamentally changed our concept of cell phones. For the first time, the cell phone had a full-fledged browser, which enabled phones to run various server-based services. But the iPhone missed one important feature: voice command. The Siri team saw this as the future feature for all phones, and a business opportunity for Siri.

For two years, the Siri team worked hard to perfect the speech recognition technology.

After iPhone allowed third-party apps, the Siri team saw a chance to showcase their technology. They uploaded Siri to the App Store in February 2010.

Within two weeks after Siri was put in the App Store, CEO Kittlaus got a call, "This is Steve Jobs. Would you like to come to my house?" Steve Jobs at his most charming self. Adam and his co-founder went to Steve Jobs' home in Palo Alto. They talked for a long time. The Siri team did not want to sell their company at that time. They had a much bigger vision of growing Siri to make it smarter and more capable. But they could not refuse Steve Jobs and his powerful persuasion. Imagine putting the device directly in a button that can be used by tens of millions of users. Instead of users searching for this obscure app, Siri would be right there with the user and be the major interface between the user and phone.

Siri became part of Apple in April 2010, and a household name was born. It first appeared in the iPhone 4 in October 2011, and became an instant sensation.

The success of Siri is a triumph of speech recognition research. While Dragon made it available for enthusiasts on the PC, Siri made it available to a much wider audience.

## Seattle, Washington, 2011

After working for four years in Microsoft, Nikko Ström embarked on a new career. In 2011, he joined Amazon, also located in Seattle. The success of Siri made Ström realize that speech recognition had become mature and could be integrated into many devices other than phones. What could be a consumer device that uses speech interface?

Ström and his colleagues put together a product plan. At Amazon, they pitched Jeff Bezos and the executive team. The plan envisioned an intelligent, voice-controlled household appliance that could play music, read the news aloud, and order groceries – all by simply letting users talk to it from anywhere in the house. It sounded almost futuristic. Amazon Vice President David Limp later said, this reminded him of the movie Star Trek, "you could be anywhere on the Starship Enterprise, and you would say the word 'computer,' and it would wake up and answer any question."

Jeff Bezos was enthusiastic. He gave the green light. The Echo project was born. It remained a secret project for several years. Ström could not tell others about it, including his wife.

The key technology challenge was recognition accuracy and speed. Between 2009 and 2011, speech recognition achieved some breakthrough. This owes to deep learning. Microsoft Speech scientist Li Deng worked with Geoffrey Hinton to prove that speech recognizers with deep neural networks could outperform previous methods on a variety of speech recognition benchmarks.

Training a deep neural network required a lot of data. Alexa was trained on thousands of hours of stored data Amazon had collected from their customers (and later millions of Alexa devices). The research team used a large-scale distributed system across 80 GPUs to train their speech recognition model. It was about 55,000 frames per second that corresponded to process about 90 minutes of recorded speech.

"Remember that a 16-year-old had heard 14,000 hours of speech, this system can process this in about three hours. We are talking about how fascinating these systems reach human parity," said Ström.

On November 6, 2014, Amazon released Echo, which became a runaway hit. In late 2015, it was the best-selling product on Amazon with price higher than $100 per unit. In 2017, over 20 million of the 33.2 million home speakers sold were Echo devices.

With Alexa, all smart home appliances in the future can respond to voice commands, and Echo plays a role as a central controller. In the meantime, Alexa enables more functionalities ranging from ordering a pizza to reading Bible verses. As of March 2018, the Alexa store, which is just like the App Store, has assembled more than 30,000 skills.

Alexa now supports three languages: English, German, and Japanese. How to apply the existing model to different languages with minimum efforts? The answer is *transfer learning*. This is a method that has been used in computer vision and speech recognition. To apply it to another language, say German, we simply train a neural network trained first in English, then use German language data to continue training the same neural network. This system would be much better than a system trained from scratch.

Another showcase of deep learning is centered around the cocktail party effect, the ability of people to focus on a single talker or conversation in a noisy environment. The Alexa team proposed an encoder-decoder model in 2016. The system first uses a recurrent neural network to extract a vector representation for the Alexa awake word (e.g., "Alexa"). Another recurrent neural network gets input from the vector representation and the features of the speech and makes its endpoint decision.

## Text-to-Speech

In the early days, computers spoke in a monotone voice. Remember the mechanical voice of early machines? Even Hal in *2001: A Space Odyssey* did not try to achieve a perfect human voice (it was thought not possible). But Alexa has such a pleasing voice that you almost take it for a human being. In order to make a computer to generate each word in a continuous and reasonable fashion, a lot of research had to be done. This included intonation, inflection, speed, and so on.

The typical steps for speech synthesis are text normalization, grapheme-to-phoneme conversion, and sound wave form generation. There is a recurrent neural network that inputs phonetic features, linguistic features, and semantic word vectors, and outputs a good target value for speech segments, including pitch, duration, and intensity. These target values can lead to searching small speech segments from the database.

Essentially, it's the reverse of speech recognition process, with some additional challenges such as intonation and smoothness of word concatenation. The field of text-to-speech (also called speech synthesis) has also become mature in the last 40 years.

As in speech recognition, the Alexa team also uses deep learning for speech synthesis.

Today, as Amazon continues to push forward advancements in speech recognition and text-to-speech technologies, Nicco Ström leads the effort as the senior principal scientist at Amazon, overseeing the Alexa team of over 100 scientists.

# 10.

## Natural Language Understanding

I used to have a big orange cat. He had long fluffy hair and always climbed up to my lap whenever I sat on the sofa. Sometimes he followed me around the house, begging for food or for me to pet him. He would jump on the desk when I worked on my computer. He would lay his body between me and the keyboard, enjoying my occasional stroke on his head. Cub was a loyal cat, always around and always affectionate. Sometimes I would to talk to him. "No, don't do that," I scolded him. He seemed to know. But he never spoke back to me. I wondered what he was thinking and how he felt.

How deeply we are wired to communicate in language. It's in words we share love, hate, encouragement, and information. It's in words that we are bonded. Consider, for example, all those beautiful words lovers say to each other.

Therefore, when Alexa appeared, I was fascinated. When I would tell her "Play Pandora Whitney Houston," Alexa needed to understand whether the term Whitney Houston referred to a singer or a channel. How would the computer know that the words "Whitney Houston" refers to a singer?

The computer searched for it in a dictionary. But the dictionary can be large, and there are some ambiguities.

This is why sometimes Alexa would ask, "Do you want to play a channel called 'Whitney Houston' in Pandora?"

Natural language understanding involves the following steps: part-of-speech tagging and named entity detection.

What is a part of speech? It is basically a category of words. In English, there are 36 categories (according to Penn Treebank data, a dataset collected by University of Pennsylvania, which labels text with tags). The first step of natural language understanding is assigning a POS tag to each word in a sentence.

For example, if we have these tags: Noun, verb, adjective, adverb, determinative, preposition, coordinator, and interjection (such as "Ah" or "ouch"), we can tag words in the following sentence as:

Play Pandora Whitney Houston.

Verb Noun Noun Noun

Once we have a word tagged, we extract entities from the sentence. Such entities could be a person, a company, a product, or a location. Since an entity is associated with a special name, it is also called a named entity. For example, the following text contains three named entities:

_Apple_ has hired _Paul Deneve_ as vice president, reporting to CEO _Tim Cook_. The first term "Apple" indicates a company, and the second and third are persons.

Named Entity Recognition (NER) is an important component in social media analysis. It helps us to understand user sentiment on specific products. NER is also important for product searches for e-commerce companies. It helps us to understand user search queries related to certain products.

To map each name to an entity, one solution is using a dictionary of special names. Unfortunately, this approach has two serious problems. The first problem is that our dictionary is not complete. New companies are created and new products are sold every day. It is hard to keep track all the new names. The second problem is the ambiguity of associating a name to an entity. The following example illustrates this:

*As Washington politicians argue about the budget reform, it is a good time to look back at George Washington's time.*

In this example, the first mention of "Washington" refers to a city, while the second mention refers to a person. The distinction of these two entities comes from their context.

To resolve ambiguity in entity mapping, we can create certain rules to utilize the context. For example, we can create the following rules:

1. When "Washington" is followed by "politician," then it refers to a city.
2. When "Washington" is preceded by "in," then it refers to a city.
3. When "Washington" is preceded by "George," then it refers to a person.

But such rules could be too many. For example, each of the following phrases would generate a different rule:

"Washington mentality," "Washington atmosphere," "Washington debate," as well as "Washington biography" and "Washington example." The richness of natural language makes the number of rules explode and still susceptible to exceptions.

Instead of manually creating rules, we can apply machine learning. The advantage of machine learning is that it creates patterns automatically from examples. No rule needs to be manually written by humans. The machine learning algorithm takes a set of training examples, and chunks out its own model (that is comparable to rules). If we get new training data, we can retrain the machine learning algorithm and generate a new model quickly.

How does the machine learning approach work?

Natural language understanding also involves mapping semantic words to categories, a dictionary, or a database. It seems trivial. After all, isn't it easy to map a word to something in our database? In fact, it is very different. The word "apple," is it a fruit or company name? The word "red," is it a color or a brand name? This problem is called named entity recognition. It involves mapping of nouns to their true meaning.

One example is product attribute extraction. One would imagine that products are well-defined, and there won't be ambiguity. But my work at eBay taught me that this problem is far from being solved. In human sentences there are:

1. Acronyms
2. Abbreviations

3. Typos

We have tried coming up with dictionary mapping combined with human rules. It simply does not work. There are too many exceptions.

Instead of relying on a limited dictionary and hand-crafted rules, we decided to apply machine learning to identify product attributes. This gave us flexibility of identifying an product attribute based on its context, regardless the typos or abbreviations.

In fact, my major mandate after joining eBay was to overhaul the rule-based system and replace it with a machine learning based approach to identify product attributes.

How do we apply machine learning? The most straightforward way is applying supervised learning. It works like this: We label every word in the sentence in terms of one of the following classes: company, brand, color, generation, or NA (none of the above). We create training data. Then we run through a machine learning method on this training data. Now every word has its context. Each word does not stand alone. We construct learning features on each word:

1. Position in the sentence.
2. Capitalized?
3. Contain a numerical number?
4. What are two words before?
5. What two words are after?

In this way, we convert a product attribution identification problem into a machine learning problem.

This approach is much more scalable. We can apply it to US products, or UK products. We can apply it to English, German, or Chinese. There is no need for a human to get involved in this process. We can accommodate acronyms or abbreviations. In other words, we don't require the brand to be certain words. All we need to do is obtain some initial training data. Then we can discover even new brand names.

There is a catch with the machine learning method we just used. It is called "supervised" learning. This requires someone to label our data for us, and our training needs to be large enough.

Human labels are hard to come by. Instead of relying on humans to label a large amount of data, how can we self-train based on a small amount of labeled data? This is called semi-supervised learning.

In our bootstrapped approach, we do not ask humans to label the data at all. Instead, we use a small dictionary of well-known brands. We then label a dataset with this dictionary by which labels are automatically generated. This is our initial training dataset. Once we train on this dataset, we apply our model to the next batch of data, and get an additional label. Then we treat this newly labeled dataset as our training set, and apply them to what we have not seen before.

Notice that there is a self-fulfilling bias here, as the initial label determines how well we classify the next dataset, it's possible that the data could have been classified incorrectly. This is the danger with most semi-supervised learning. This problem has not been completely solved. In practice, semi-supervised learning works very well, and has given us good results.

Ultimately, we would like to achieve unsupervised learning, where the system can tell whether something is a product attribute just by processing the sentence.

When I was a student at University of Michigan, I listened to a fascinating talk by Professor John Laird. John was the head of our AI lab. He posed this challenge in his talk:

With the sentence: "John saw a woman in a park with a telescope," do we know if John is with a telescope, or the woman is with a telescope?

This question puzzled me for a long time. If we design a computer program to parse this sentence, how would a computer know which interpretation is right?

Today, I realized there are two possible ways to answer this question, and each represent a different approach in AI camp.

When expert system dominates the AI field, people try to resolve this ambiguity with a knowledge base. Suppose someone has entered the fact that to "see" someone far away requires a telescope? This approach turns out to be not scalable. How can we encode all the human knowledge into a system, in a format where it remains consistent? The failure of the Cyc Project (see Chapter 4 on rule-based systems) showed that it is almost impossible.

With statistical parsing, if we see more examples where "telescope" is always at the end of sentences and it is always associated with the first word of the sentence, then we assign telescope to John.

The problem with the statistical approach is that we don't have enough examples in the beginning. How would the system know? There is where learning comes in. We start with no bias, assuming each meaning is equally possible. As the system is given feedback, for example, the right answer is "John" is with a telescope, then we increase the probability of assigning telescope to John to say 0.7, and 0.3 to the woman. The next example associates "telescope" with the woman, then we reduce the probability of John to say 0.6, and 0.4 to the woman. Note that how much we change the probability depends on which machine learning method we use. When data samples are large enough, the probability assignment from different methods should stay the same.

Therefore, our system is agnostic regarding how we parse a sentence, and it keeps an open mind when new evidence is introduced. This is the power of machine learning. It trusts only what it sees. Here, human knowledge of whether a person who wants to see far away needs a telescope is not that important any more. Machine learning removes the need for human input and it trains on data.

*** 

Roger Schank is super smart and charismatic. He pioneered the Natural Language Processing field in the

1970s and 1980s. He tried to tackle the language understanding problem by applying world knowledge, represented by rules. But this approach didn't work that well, as was the case with all rule-based systems. Then Schank invented case-based reasoning, which is a semi-machine learning method, and fascinated me when I started my research on machine learning. But Schank was bitterly disappointed with the slow progress of NLP. Looking back, the computing power was not sufficient then, and there was not enough data to use. Schank wanted more action. He took big funding ($30 million at that time) and hired 25 of his colleagues from Yale, who all joined him to settle down in Northwestern University to build educational software. He still supervised graduate students.

In the summer 1995, I met him when I was interviewing for the PhD program at Northwestern University.

I walked into a new building where there were a lot of young people and exciting posters. It felt vibrant, but a little commercial (later I recognized this is what a typical startup feels). I had heard of Schank from AI classes, and I felt both excited and trepid to see him in person. He sat in a big office behind an enormous desk. He looked at me casually as I walked. After I sat down, he asked, "So you want to study PhD in AI. What's your goal of studying AI?" I knew Schank had devoted his life to NLP and I was a big fan of Eliza, so I blurted it out, "I want to build something like Eliza." I intended to say that I wanted to create a real AI program that talked like Eliza, not the current pattern matching method.

Before I could go further, Schank snarled, "That's not realistic." He eyed me with disappointment. "In research, we have to be realistic," he added. I was surprised and puzzled. Did he mean, by "realistic," giving up that dream to turn to software? (At that time commercial software had only simple menus and no AI components.) Then how would we push forward in AI to eventually fulfill Turing's dream? (I was all enthusiastic to continue to push for Turing's dream and Eliza seemed the best testbed for tackling that problem.)

While Schank left AI research, his students continued. Gerald DeJong continued the work at University of Illinois at Urbana Champaign. DeJong invented explanation based learning, which tried to learn rules from data. He influenced his student Raymond Mooney. In the 1990s, Mooney was a rising star in NLP, who introduced the statistical approach, or machine learning, into natural language processing. His work of processing medical literature used machine learning to extract the names of new drugs and new proteins. This generated a lot of interest.

The statistical approach, or machine learning approach, is a big paradigm shift for NLP. If we simply count statistics to see if something is a drug name or person name, does that mean the computer "understands" it is a drug? The older AI researchers shook their heads. They felt this deviated from real understanding. But the field NLP has seen the rise of the statistical approach and its power. A good indicator of this is the papers presented at the ACL (Association of Computer Linguistics) conference. In 1990, only 12.8% used the statistical approach. By 1997, that number was 63.5%. By the middle of the early-2000s, the ACL conference was dominated by the machine learning approach.

\*\*\*

Natural language understanding (NLP) is still an evolving domain. By applying NLP to processing text documents, we can extract user sentiments on social media, for example, how many tweets are positive and how many are negative about a product. We can automatically identify trendy topics in the news. For example, if 10,000 bloggers are reporting on different subjects, can Google News identify what's the hottest topic now? If 100 million tweets are posted each day, can Twitter or anyone monitoring Twitter posts figure out what are the trendy topics?

We interact with a lot of written text in our daily life. Text data includes news, our legal documents, and our inventions (patent documents). We communicate via email and SMS using text, we create text documents at work, we write blogs to share our learning and emotion. Our lives are impacted by how we consume and understand all the text in front of us. Understanding text data could impact our financial future (a company working on risk analysis, or using Twitter sentiment to predict stock). As we are inundated by such large volumes of text information, computer programs that can digest it for us become very valuable.

In addition, the computer can be smarter, giving us insight that we have not seen before.

Mining human text is like mining a collective brain. There is so much wisdom that comes from people, and so many insights. But people's opinions are diverse. Yet, through voting on IMDB (Intern Movie Data Base), we get to know what movies are more interesting to watch. Through user reviews, we know what products are popular.

Today, deep learning has revolutionized the field of NLP. Our ability to understand text, asking questions and getting answers, and even creating stories by computer, has reached unprecedented sophistication. We have reached a golden age of natural language processing.

# 11.

## Dialog Systems

When Alexa tells me about my schedule, she pauses and asks, "Do you want to hear more?" When I say "yes," she continues to read out my remaining meetings.

Alexa is a dialog system, which makes it fundamentally different from other systems such as "question-answering" or voice search systems. In a question-answering system, you ask a question, the system then answers. It's a one-shot interaction. The system does not link your current questions with previous ones you asked. Similarly, in "voice search" where each query is treated as brand new, the system does not remember what you asked before

A dialog system remembers previous conversations and uses them as context to respond in the next round of questioning. This is fundamentally different from other one-shot system.

What is inside a dialog system? How do we build it?

A dialog system has the following components:

- Dialog manager
- Speech recognizer (if it is speech interface)

- Natural language understanding (parser, named entity recognizer)
- Knowledge base

The central component of a dialog system is the dialog manager. This is the brain of a dialog system. The dialog manager manages the flow of the dialog. Whenever a dialog starts, it tries to fulfill the main tasks a user asks.

For chatterbots (text chat), we can do away with the speech recognizer and text-to-speech. But the core components remain the same.

The flow of a dialog goes through the following steps:

Semantic understanding ⊠ User intention ⊠ Information retrieval (action)

For example, in a simple command "Alexa, play urban chill for me." Alexa needs to understand it is a request to play music.

In dialog management, we are trying to get user intention. Is it for information, or play, or just making conversation? Suppose there are 100 things we can do for the user, which of the things does the user want? What if the user is just making a comment?

In general, we can divide user intention into the following aspects:

- Action request (Play a song, etc.)
- Information requests (Why is the sky blue?)
- Trivial comments (Why can't you understand me?)

These are called speech acts. There are about eight basic speech acts:

1. Request
2. Statement
3. Yes/No Question
4. Confirmation

For example, "Play a song for me" is a request. But "I don't like this song" is a statement.

When a user asks, "Are you a human?", it is a "Yes/No" question.

In each specific dialog system, we will have dialog acts, which are specialized speech acts, adopted to a domain. For example, in the music domain, we have:

- Request for songs
- Question on album name

How do we classify user utterance into certain dialog acts? We can hand code them as rules. But it requires a lot of human knowledge and the rules may not be consistent. I had some personal experience on this.

In the mid early-2000s, I worked in Bosch Research's language group. We were designing an in-car dialog system.

We had a big Honda van. Our group used to drive it around to show how a car could talk when it is driving. This was 2007, before Siri, before Google Voice, and long before Alexa. Our mission was to build and make the car act on the driver's command while they drove. It was an exciting time.

One day the big boss from Germany was coming to visit. "Let's do a test drive," my manager said.

What's more fun than seeing it in action? We had a big laptop sitting in the trunk, connecting to a microphone in front of the steering wheel, and a small screen showing what the computer spoke back and what it recognized.

The car could do a few things: play music, navigate, play the radio, and search for local restaurants. In building a music recognizer, we used Gracenote, which was the largest collection of artists and song names. But it also posed challenges, as there are duplications of names. This posed a challenge for a speech recognizer (in its language model), and ultimately for the natural language understanding unit.

My main task was revising the dialog manager into a scalable system. The system was originally written by a few graduate students at Stanford University. It consisted of a lot of rules. I stared at those rules with dismay, as there were so many rules and it was hard to know if they were all correct. My first task was converting this manager into a machine-learning based system.

The original rule-based system had a lot of sentence patterns. For example, a "Where do I ...?" is captured as query (question).

Learning about user intention requires data. This could be a previous utterance that user have confirmed, and Alexa's action was correct before.

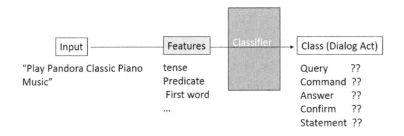

Figure 11.1: A Dialog Manager

The classifier can be any supervised learning methods mentioned before: decision tree, SVM, or logistic regression. But you can also think of using deep learning if the data are large enough.

Alexa first needed to classify user input into one of these intentions. There are way more variations of trivial questions than serious commands (which Amazon limits to certain phrases).

This is where chatterbot development comes in handy.

For a dialog system to speak back to the user, the first step is to quickly check against common requests and trivia questions, such as "Who are you?" or "Where were you born?" There is a lot of computing going on in this first step. (It could be machine-learning based classification, trained over many user utterances.)

Once the intention is identified, Alexa needs to execute the action. Assuming the user has serious intention other than trivial comments, Alexa needs to understand the specific action the user requests. This requires understanding the meaning of the words. This understanding is what we mean by natural language processing. "Play a song" may be different from "play Pandora." Note one is a specific song, and the other is a station. Each would lead to a different action from Alexa. In the first part, Alexa needs to retrieve the last song the user listened to, or play a song in the similar genre. In the second, it is only playing a station so the action is simpler.

Mapping a song name to the actual song to retrieve is the part where rubber meets the road. If we retrieve the wrong song, then the user is not happy. This is why Alexa pronounces the action while doing it. For example, after I request her to play Pandora, she will say "Playing your last Pandora station." while starting the music.

Matching user requests to databases involves search indexing, where millions of song names are all indexed in a database for quick retrieval.

A dialog system is useful for technical support, where it can ask the user for information bit by bit. It is also useful for general customer support, where a system can talk interactively with the user.

Alexa is adding many skills nowadays: she can schedule meetings, search for local movies, and read a Bible verse.

Can Alexa really understand us, making conversation with us? Would she be funny, smart, and well informed like "her" in the movie *Her*? In the movie, the program talks to our main character, the single lonely man. She is humorous, understanding, and possesses emotional empathy. She helps him to write a love letter, to have an adventure, and to enjoy life.

I really want an Alexa who can send email on my behalf, remind me of my daily walking, order foods for me when I need them, and essentially become my personal assistant. In other words, I want an Alexa who is proactive, taking initiative to do things simply because she knows my habits and my needs.

How far are we from that reality? Google Chat and Facebook Messenger are two programs attempting this. And popping up more and more frequently are many "personal assistant" startup companies. We expect personal assistant programs to succeed in some specific domains: customer support, food ordering, scheduling, and even knowledge advising. You can imagine an advisor on travel, home repair, astronomy, or even healthy eating. Such an advisor would have a conversation with you almost like a real person.

Can we build a general purpose program that can answer any question that we may have? While Google Search is bringing human knowledge to our fingertips, it is different from having an in-depth conversation that explores our particular needs and wishes.

For example, in a conversational system, suppose you want to talk to someone about traveling to Australia for a week. This involves general understanding of your main goal, what to see, and your budget and time constraints. Imagine you are talking to smart local guide while in Australia. This person could give you a lot of advice on what to do, and what not to do. Suppose you have a personal assistant who fetches this information and arranges your trip for you based on your schedule. This could make your life so easy. Your conversation will be with such a travel assistant, who understands your needs: "outdoor activities that are not strenuous" means easy hikes, or "relaxed dinner night" means a restaurant that has the right ambience and is quiet.

As more AI assistants are built, in chat programs, in mobile apps, or carrying a physical body like speaker or robots, knowing the technology behind them could give you power. This may change very soon as today's computer programs can learn from millions of chat transcripts. A computer program can memorize and speak back like a human. For example, imagine a computer offers comforting words when it knows you are sad, or it organizes your files without your asking, and schedules meetings for you by checking your calendar. These are personal assistant programs and they are beginning to regularly show up our lives.

# 12.

## The Age of Big Data

In 1999, Jeff Dean arrived at a small startup in Palo Alto, California. There were only 19 people in the company then. The company was Google. Employees were crammed in a few small offices in Palo Alto's outskirt East Bayshore Road (before the company moved to its current campus in Mountain View). Despite how crowded it was, everyone got free food, big jars of candies, and free drinks. The place was full of excitement.

Three years before this Jeff Dean came to live in sunny California, fresh from his PhD life at University of Washington. He joined DEC's Research Lab in Palo Alto, working on compilers – translating source code into a language that a computer can readily execute.

Dean was attracted by Google's ambition of processing all the information in the world. Dean arrived at the right time, when the 1-year-old company started to expand. Massive data requires massive computing infrastructure. The company was looking for a solution at that time that could scale its system so it could process terabytes of data quickly and efficiently. Jeff Dean made significant contributions to bring Google to scale.

In 2004, Dean and his collaborator Sanjay Ghemawat released their paper on MapReduce, a programming model for processing and generating large data sets. This incorporated parallelization, fault tolerance, data distribution, and load balancing. The MapReduce system can run on thousands of machines clustered into a network and distribute data to each node in the network. It has two steps: In the Map step the code is passed to the nodes in the cluster. Each node processes the data that is stored locally on that node. If a node fails, it is detected and the task is re-assigned to another node on the system. In the Reduce step the results from different machines are collected and combined.

MapReduce was used to regenerate Google's index of the World Wide Web completely. It replaced the old ad hoc programs that updated the index and ran the various analyses. MapReduce was quickly recognized as a revolutionary work for early big data workloads and became an industry-wide solution.

Then in 2006, they published "Bigtable: A Distributed Storage System for Structured Data." Bigtable is a distributed storage system for managing structured data designed to scale to a very large size: petabytes of data across thousands of commodity servers. Bigtable is used in many of Google's products.

MapReduce and the new file system spawned Hadoop, an open-source framework created by Yahoo! engineers. From 2007 to 2014 Hadoop was the dominating big data processing system.

Hadoop had its unique Highly Distributed File System (HDFS), which is different from a traditional file system. Consider how the traditional computer handles files: The file is stored on a disk for reading and writing, and the disk has a pointer to the beginning of the file.

HDFS changed this concept. Your file was no longer stored in one place, but a location assigned by a name server. This name server assigned your file to a computer that was one of many (could be hundreds of thousands).

With Hadoop, we no longer had to worry about the limitation of storage on one computer. We can infinitely expand our storage capacity by adding more computers to the cluster.

I remember trying to process some user log data for the first time after I joined eBay. Very quickly my laptop was filled with 200 gigabytes of data, and my smart Python code now ran so slowly. I waited patiently for hours, but had to give up. It was just insane to go through such large data sequentially. Why not divide them into chunks and process them parallelly?

This explains why we all moved toward distributed computing. Big data made distributed computing, or cloud computing, inevitable.

Since the invention of World Wide Web, data has grown exponentially. On the web, all user activities are recorded. The link you clicked, the page you visited, the information you entered, the devices you used to connect, and the search engine you used for the visit. We know a lot more about the users. In other words, browsing and purchases leave a trail of data. We call this a web log. Mining web logs is the fundamental part of data mining. It is behind e-commence recommendation, keyword search recommendation, and search ranking.

In addition to user activity data (search and purchase), we also have a lot of text data written by the users. This can be user reviews, blogs, forum posts, and social media data. On top of that, we have data on products, such as movies as they are available to sell on the web. This generates rich image data and product.

Furthermore, we have social networks that tells us who is connected to whom, LinkedIn uses this to recommend candidates, and Facebook uses this to recommend restaurants that your friends like. Twitter uses this to recommend news that could be interesting to both you and people you follow. Such data are connected in a network, which we can graph. Graph data mining has become very popular and powerful in recent times.

With smart phones and cheap memory, we have seen an explosion of image data and video data. Mining such data can give us much more information. From video surveillance, to security, to house design.

Most recently, the Internet of things has taken data generation to the next level. Imagine sensors attached to every light, every microwave, and every speaker. Imagine these devices sending data to the cloud 24/7. We are at the dawn of data explosion and cloud computing is just in its infancy.

If there is one person who has contributed more than anyone else to the modern day of big data and its coming revolution. It's Jeff Dean.

Growing up in a family with parents who were tropical disease researchers, Dean moved frequently – from Minnesota to Hawaii, then to Geneva, Uganda, Somalia, and back to the States. Dean had a very international childhood.

Dean was attracted to computers at a very young age. He developed his programming skills by writing software for analyzing a large amount of epidemiological data, which he claimed was "26 times faster" than the industry-wide software. The Centers for Disease Control adopted his software and translated it into 13 languages.

In 1990, Dean received his bachelor's degree from University of Minnesota. In his senior thesis, he touched upon neural network training and modern development of AI, and wrote parallel training codes for neural networks in C language. The paper "Parallel Implementation of Neural Network Training: Two Back-Propagation Approaches" proposed two methods for training neural networks.

After his bachelor's degree, Dean worked for a year for the World Health Organization's Global Program on AIDS, developing software to do statistical modeling, forecasting, and analysis of the HIV pandemic. He then went back to graduate school and got his PhD from University of Washington, before he eventually joined Google.

Even though he is a superb engineer and helped Google to scale in the early 2000s, Dean's PhD training eventually led him back to research, and eventually to lead the AI effort at Google.

This all started with a chance meeting with Andrew Ng, a Stanford professor, in 2011. (See Chapter 12 for the story.)

# 13.

## Deep Learning

In the same year (1987) Hinton joined the University of Toronto, a smart young post-doc came to join him from France. His name is Yann LeCun. LeCun had just gotten his PhD from Pierre and Marie Curie University in Paris. His PhD dissertation independently discovered the backpropagation algorithm as Hinton and others had done a year earlier.

After working with Hinton for a year, LeCun joined Bell Lab in New Jersey as a researcher. In 1989, LeCun published a paper titled "Backpropagation applied to handwritten zip code recognition." In this paper, he invented the first convolutional neural network.

A convolutional neural network (CNN or ConvNet) uses "convolution" to transform one layer to another layer. In mathematics, convolution refers to applying a function g to an existing function f, to achieve a transformation of f (a new shape). The operation of "convolution" in a CNN applies filters (also called kernels) to the previous layer. A filter is a square matrix, with size ranging from 2 x 2 to 11 x 11 or larger (typically the filter size is less than 5 x 5).

For example, when applying a filter of 5 x 5 to the original image, we map every region of size 5 x 5 in the original picture to a single point in the new image. Below is the picture to illustrate this:

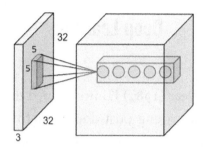

Figure 13.1: Illustration of filter applied to images

The original image has a size of 32 x 32. After mapping, a region of 5 x 5 in the first layer becomes a point in the next layer.

In the first convolutional neural network by LeCun, the input layer is an image size of 16 x 16. After applying a 5 x 5 filter to the original 16 x 16 image, the first hidden layer becomes an image of 8 x 8. The second hidden layer applies a 5 x 5 filter to the previous layer, resulting an image size of 4 x 4. Thus convolution shrinks the original image, extracting the main features from the original picture.

The invention of CNN did not get much attention then. LeCun continued to refine his work. After nine years, in 1998, Yann LeCun and his colleagues (including Yoshua Bengio) at AT&T Lab published another paper that applied CNN to recognizing documents (letters and digits in a document, thus becoming the foundation of a document scanner).

The convolutional operation in that 1998 paper combined three ideas: local receptive field (filter), shared weights within the same layer, and subsampling. This preserved recognition invariance despite shift, scale, and distortion. The specific architecture they proposed was LeNet-5. (It's numbered 5 because some other LeNet structures were tried before.) Each filter was still of size 5 x 5.

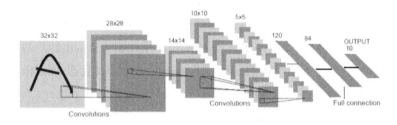

Figure 13.2: LeNet-5, a Convolution Neural Network in 1998

LeNet-5 has a total six hidden layers: two convolutional layers, two subsampling layers and two fully connected layers. Thus, the network gets deep whereas it's deep learning, meaning learning that is happening via neural networks of more than two hidden layers.

The 1998 paper received increased attention, and convolutional neural networking started to become more recognized. But the adoption was very small. The main difficulty was in training a deep neural network. LeNet-5 has 1024 input nodes, and 4704 nodes in the first hidden layer, which means there are more than 4 million weights connecting (neurons in) the first layer to the (neurons in) the second layer. Updating these weights requires a lot of training data and significant computer power. Researchers had to wait weeks before a neural network was fully trained (all weights are updated based on training examples).

This situation changed after 2006 when Hinton published two papers on how to speed up deep learning.

For two decades (from 1987 to 2006), after moving to University of Toronto, Hinton continued to push the advancement of neural networks. The Internet Age has seen many people use machine learning, but mostly decision tree and SVM. It seemed that neural networks were outdated. But Hinton believed in the power of neural networks. He realized the main difficulty of using this method was the training speed. In 2006, Hinton published two papers "A Fast Learning Algorithm for Deep Belief Nets" and "Reducing the Dimensionality of Data with Neural Networks." Hinton showed that it's possible to learn deep neural networks much faster. This excited a lot of researchers.

Hinton's paper started the era of deep learning, where a lot of researchers started to explore the properties of deep neural networks, and found ways to make training faster. One of the researchers was Andrew Ng, a professor at Stanford University.

Andrew Ng got his PhD from UC Berkeley, studying under Michael Jordan. Jordan had worked with Hinton back in the 1980s at UC Dan Diego, helping to revive the field of neural networks. Ng did a lot of pioneering work during his graduate study. He wrote papers on statistical machine learning ("On Spectral Clustering: Analysis and an Algorithm"), generative probabilistic model ("On LDA Model (Latent Drichlet Allocation), "co-authored with David Blei and Michael Jordan), unsupervised learning, and reinforcement learning ("Algorithms for Inverse Reinforcement Learning," co-authored the paper with Stuart Russell). The most influential was the "On LDA Model," which assumes hidden distribution of topics of documents. This model has been widely used for unsupervised document classification.

But Ng was unsatisfied with LDA. He wanted to find a more general approach, with deeper foundation. In 2002, Ng joined Stanford University as an assistant professor. He started to pay attention to deep learning. By 2006, it was clear to him, there was some magic about deep learning. Ng put almost all of his PhD students in deep learning research. His student Honglak Lee studied image recognition with deep belief networks. Another student Richard Socher applied deep learning to natural language processing, summarizing sentiments from online posts.

\*\*\*

Andrew Ng came to eBay to give a talk. The big conference room was filled with people. It was 2011. We were excited about all the data and machine learning at eBay. "What are you going to talking about?" I asked Andrew before inviting him over to Stanford. "I will cover the future possibility of deep learning," he replied. *I have tried to use neural networks but found it too slow. Could it ever be practical?* I wondered.

Machine learning was already demonstrating its versatility at that time. From decision trees to support-vector machines, we were seeing how it can quickly summarize data. I thought we had all the tools we needed then.

Andrew was a good speaker. His talk was very engaging. With pictures and case studies, he showed that the same type of computer algorithm can be used to recognize images, speech, and natural language. It was magical. We were infected by his enthusiasm.

***

In 2011, Ng became a consultant for Google and started a project with Jeff Dean called Project Marvin. The goal was to try out the deep learning approach leveraging Google's massive amount of data and compute. Ng brought in his PhD student Quoc Le. Together with Jeff Dean and another Google researcher, they formed the beginning team of Google Brain.

In 2012, Quoc Le (Le as the first author, with other authors from Google Brain) published the famous cat paper ("Building High-level Features Using Large Scale Unsupervised Learning"), which presented a trained deep neural network model that could recognize a cat based on 10 million digital images taken from YouTube videos, as well as over 3,000 objects in the ImageNet dataset. The model, which contained one billion synapses, 100 times larger than anyone who had ever tried, was trained on 1,000 machines (16,000 cores).

When the paper was presented at ICML 2012 (International Conference on Machine Learning), there was a big stir. The feasibility of deep learning was finally proven, given enough data and large computing power.

But how well does deep learning perform relative to other machine learning methods? This question was answered by Geoff Hinton's group, also in the year 2012. Hinton's PhD students Alex Krizhevsky and Ilya Sutskever participated in the ImageNet competition and won first place.

The ImageNet competition started in 2010, with 1.2 million labeled images for training, and 150,000 for testing. The goal is to classify these images into 1,000 categories. The winning team in 2010 used a sparse-coding model and many features. These features are hand-coded, thus requiring a lot of knowledge on image processing. This is a classical way to approach computer vision.

Hinton's group used just raw images without any human-coded features. Instead, they let the neural network learn image features automatically. They used two GPUs and seven hidden layers. The first five layers are convolution operation (similar to LeCun's work), and the last two layers are simple neurons (fully connected).

The input layer is the image 224 x 224 x 3. The first convolution layer uses an 11 x 11 filter, and the resulting image has a size of 55 x 55. The next layer reduces the image size to 27 x 27. The third convolutional layer uses a 5 x 5 filter and further reduces the image size to 13 x 13.

This network has 650,000 neurons and 60 million parameters (weights).

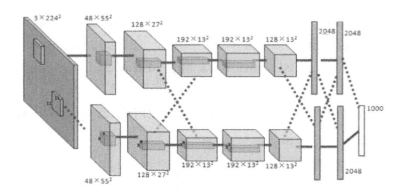

Figure 13.3: The architecture of AlexNet

Such a performance was unheard of. The beauty of this is there was no human involvement. No one designed the "features." The computer used raw pixels, and learned the weights inside the network by examples.

The field of computer vision has spent the last 40 years trying to crack the code of understanding features. They thought of many ingenious way to understand a picture: color, histogram, saturation, sharpness, location, etc. A computer vision researcher would spend a decade to build his expertise. Overnight, that expertise was overtaken by a computer that had no knowledge of vision. It started from scratch, taking in training data (labeled pictures) one by one, and then gradually learning to recognize the right object. The world was amazed. What was the magic of this approach? It turned out the convolution in the first five layers are the key. Each convolution layer uses 48 filters to extract different features from the previous layer. One filter captures sharpness, another filter extracts diagonal features, and so on. So people ask "How do we define those filters?" The beauty is that you don't need to define filters. Each filter (the weights) is automatically learned by observing the data.

A convolutional neural network shrinks the picture smaller and smaller, and each time only extract the most important features from the previous pictures. After a few layers, you get the most important feature left, the category "cat," "boat," or "person," etc. The convolution, or transformation based on a filter, is the key in this process. The automatically learned filter is the power of this neural network. Therefore, there is no need for human involvement. The only catch is that you need a lot of training data.

At the NIPS conference 2012, Hinton and his students published the paper "Imagenet Classification with Deep Convolutional Neural Networks" (co-authored by Alex Krizhevsky, Ilya Sutskever, and Geoff Hinton). Since then, CNN has become the dominating architecture for image analysis, and has been applied to many other domains. The architecture laid out in this paper has since been called AlexNet.

The year 2012 was a watershed year for deep learning. The triumph of big data and big computing combined with undisputable superior performance put deep learning on the center stage. The world suddenly woke up to something magical.

The success of AlexNet made CNN popular and many researchers and practitioners today still use AlexNet for their CNN implementation.

The winner of the 2013 ImageNet competition was ZFNet (the winning team was Zeiler and Fergus, thus the name ZF). They used the same architecture as AlexNet, except with a smaller filter size (7 x 7) on the first convolution layer. They reduced the error rate to 15%, about 2% in error reduction.

The winner in 2014 was the Google team, and the architecture they used was called GoogleNet. GoogleNet has 22 layers. It looks like this:

Figure 13.4: GoogleNet

It introduced the *inception architecture* that uses *inception modules*. Each inception module is a small neural network by itself. Therefore, the inception architecture is a "network in network." In addition, GoogleNet uses a technique called R-CNN (Regions with CNN features), which detect regions in an image and classify them with CNN. GoogleNet achieves error rate around 6.7%, significantly lower than the previous year's error rate.

In 2015, Kaiming He and his colleagues from Microsoft won the ImageNet competition with their Residual Network (ResNet) model. It had 152 layers, and it achieved a 3.6% error rate, cutting the previous error rate by half.

As we can see, the size of the CNN has gone from eight layers in the original AlexNet in 2012 to more than 100 layers (in ResNet) in 2015. More layers require more training data, and more computing machines. Given the rapid increase of data, and more powerful GPU machines, it is now possible for all of us to adopt the more powerful CNN models.

You don't need to understand features or abstraction methods at all. All you need to do is feed the original pixels to the computer. Then computer will build its internal layers that mimic our abstraction in our brain. Then the computer will give you results that are much more accurate than if we used the human designed features.

But there is a catch with regard to deep learning. With all of its magic power, it requires a vast amount of training data. The neural network has millions of internal weights that need to learned and trained. This means millions of data points are required. Do we have this many data? If you are a web or mobile company, you may have. You get the data from users. This is why Google and Amazon Echo continue to become better. All the user data are collected and used as training data to improve speech accuracy.

The early Google Brain team built a large-scale deep learning software system, DistBelief, on top of Google's cloud computing infrastructure of hundreds of thousands of CPU cores. This enables training deep neural networks with billions of parameters. DistBelief, became the precursor to TensorFlow, the most widely used deep learning tool today.

For large companies, the internal data has been growing rapidly. The data storage becomes cheaper and data process tools becomes widely available. This makes adopting deep learning inevitable.

The second exciting domain of deep learning is speech. This is the domain where AI researchers have struggled for a long time. Hinton has worked with Microsoft researchers to build the first successful speech recognition system based on deep learning.

After image and speech, deep learning is now used in natural language processing, from machine translation to chatbots. The next frontier is general text understanding, where a computer can read an article, summarizing its content for you. A computer can write an essay like a person does.

We are in a new era of AI, where deep learning is rapidly taking over all other methods in AI. Deep learning has since become the synonym to AI in many people's minds. This will become more true in the next few years.

Hinton has become a superstar now in the AI field. It used to be that he was shunned in the mainstream AI conferences. Now he is a sought-after speaker everywhere.

"We ceased to be the lunatic fringe. We're now the lunatic core," Geoff Hinton chuckled, betraying the loneliness of someone who has defied the odds, pursuing a subject for the last four decades. As a famous author once put it, "Nothing is more powerful than an idea whose time has come." The time for Geoff Hinton's idea has finally come.

# 14.

## Reinforcement Learning

### Amherst, Massachusetts, 1982

Richard Sutton, a young man in his mid-20s, was engaged in an animated conversation with a man in early 30s, his PhD advisor Andrew Barton. They were talking about how to build an intelligent robot that behaves like a human.

Barton had a deep interest in control theory, in how machines could be programmed to react to the environment. This was useful for early robotics, where robotic arms could be used inside factories. There were also attempts to apply control theory to mobile robots. But, how could we build the decision making into a robot? Humans make decisions by looking a few steps ahead, or even far into the future. They then create a plan based on that information. Couldn't an AI robot do the same thing?

Richard Sutton thought differently. He studied animals in his undergraduate study as psychology major at Stanford University. He observed adaptive behavior of animals and was interested in building that behavior into a robot. A robot should be able to learn to change its behavior based on feedback from the environment, and not ignore long-term consequences at the same time.

It turned out Richard Bellman at Rand Institute (who overlapped with Allen Newell) published a paper in 1953 on this subject which was later called "Bellman Equation." In this paper, Bellman proposed that when a person chooses the best action to maximize the long-term payoff, it is equivalent to choosing a best action for today and then following the best long-term strategy afterwards.

The collaboration between Sutton and Barton led to the idea of reinforcement learning. But it is not a simple reinforcement learning like animals reacting to rewards or punishments. The intelligent agent cares about the long-term payment. Thus, it's interested in the impact of its current action on the long-term payoff. But how does it know the impact? This requires the agent to record the long-term payoff. This is what we call value function.

When the agent observes a reward, it updates its value function, which records the change. This is called temporal difference learning, and it was invented by Sutton and Barton in 1982. This started the early age of reinforcement learning.

In 1984, Richard Sutton wrote his PhD dissertation titled "Temporal Credit Assignment in Reinforcement Learning." It formally explained temporal difference learning. But this work did not receive much attention from the AI community until Sutton published the article "Learning to

Predict by the Methods of Temporal Differences" in *Machine Learning Journal* in 1988.

At nearly the same time, Chris Watkin at Cambridge University wrote his PhD dissertation on Q-learning in 1989. Modern reinforcement learning was born.

Reinforcement learning is not just reacting to a stimulus. An intelligent agent should be smarter than that. It should remember what it learns, and next time choose the right action. Therefore, reinforcement learning is a misleading term. More accurately it would be called "long-term reward learning through trial and error."

The framework describing the world, used by control theory, is a Markov decision process. It changes from one state to the next state, but only the most recent state impacts the next state. Markov process is the foundation of modern statistics and control theory, and later AI. In speech recognition, we use the Hidden Markov model. In natural language processing, we use the Markov process to model word sequence, where the current word depends only on its previous word.

Assuming the world follows the Markov decision process, the agent moves from one state to the next state, and gathers its rewards along the way. The long-term reward is the total payoff we will get.

But how does an agent remember its total payoffs and decide on the best action?

The long-term reward is learned when an agent interacts with an environment through many trials and errors. The robot that is running through the maze remembers every wall it hits. In the end, it remembers the previous actions that lead to dead ends. It also remembers the path (that is, a sequence of actions) that leads it successfully through the maze. The essential goal of reinforcement learning is learning a sequence of actions that lead to a long-term reward. An agent learns that sequence by interacting with the environment and observing the rewards in every state.

Q-learning is a commonly used reinforcement learning method, which tries to learn Q-value, the long-term value of an action. The learning of Q-values is done through observations.

Let's look at this example: A robot starts from the lower left corner, trying to reach the exit of a maze.

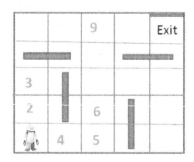

Figure 14.1: A robot learns about the path in a maze

Each location (state) is indicated by a number. There are four action choices (left, right, up, down), but in certain states, action choices are limited. For example, in state 1 (initial state), the robot has only two action choices: up, right. In state 4, it has three action choices: left, right, and up.

When the robot hits a wall, it receives reward -1. When it reaches an open location, it receives reward 0. When it reaches the exit, it receives reward 100. However, note that this one-time reward is very different from Q-values. In fact, we have Q(state, action) as:

Q(4, left) = 0.8 x 0+ 0.2 (0+0.9 Q(1,right)) and

Q(4, right) = 0.8 x 0+ 0.2 (0+0.9 Q(5,up))

Here the learning rate is 0.2 and discount rate is 0.9. The learning rate is a number between 0 and 1. It is a weight given to the new information versus the old information. The new long-term reward is the current reward, $r$, plus all future rewards in the next state, and later states, assuming this agent always takes its best actions in the future. The future rewards are discounted by a discount rate between 0 and 1, meaning future rewards are not as valuable as the reward now.

The best action in State 1 is right, and the best action in State 5 is up. Since we discount future awards, we discount the longer route (steps) to reach the goal. Thus Q(5, up) has a higher value than Q(1, right). Similarly, Q(4, right) has a higher value than Q(4, left). The best action in State 4 is going right.

Q-learning requires the agent try many times to visit all possible state-action pairs. Only then does the agent have a complete picture of the world. Q-values represent the optimal values when taking the best sequence of actions. This sequence of actions is also called policy.

A fundamental question we face is: Is it possible for an agent to learn all the Q-values when it explores the actions possible in a given environment? In other words, is such learning feasible? The answer is yes if we assume the world responds to actions. In other words, the state changes based on an action. This assumption is called the Markov Decision Process (MDP). It assumes that the next state depends on the previous state and the action taken.

Based on this assumption, all possible states can eventually be visited, and the long-term value (Q-value) of every state-action pair can be determined.

Imagine that we live in a random universe where our action has no impact on what happens next, then reinforcement learning (Q-learning) would break down. After many times of trying, we'd have to throw in the towel. Fortunately, our universe is much more predictable. When a Go player (the Go game will be discussed later in the chapter) puts down a piece on the board, the board position is clear in the next round. Our agent interacts with the environment and shapes it through its actions. The exact impact of our agent's action on the state is typically straightforward. The new state is immediately observable. The robot can tell where it ends up.

Sutton graduated in 1984. He worked as a post-doc with Barton for a year, then joined GTE as a researcher, and stayed there for nine years.

In 1992, Gerald Tesauro at IBM, inspired by Sutton's work, decided to build a system that played backgammon with temporal difference learning. He implemented this algorithm in a neural network. Tesauro's program achieved close to the level of the world champion, and beat human players.

After hearing of Tesauro's feat and the newly invented Q-learning, which Sutton considered as a special case of temporal difference learning, he was greatly encouraged. The job in the GTE industrial lab wasn't necessarily the one Sutton wanted. He communicated this to his former advisor Andrew Barton, and was encouraged to come back to work at the university. Sutton loved research, and wanted to devote his whole time to it, not bothered by corporate management.

In 1995, Sutton went back to UMass at Amhert as a research scientist. This position allowed him to supervise PhD students. His first student was Doina Precup.

***

I saw him in the lounge area. He wore blue jeans, had long hair, and looked like a hippie, unlike any professor I knew.

It was the summer of 1997, I was attending the Annual Conference on Machine Learning (ICML). The night before, my roommate at the conference, a tall and pretty graduate student named Doina asked me to meet this person, her PhD advisor.

Doina was tall, slender, pretty, and very energetic. The first night we met, we immediately hit it off. We talked about our studies and our backgrounds. She came from Romania, where she was working on her PhD for the University of Massachusetts at Amherst. I asked about what she worked on, she said, "reinforcement learning." I asked, "What is that?" I had not heard of this term before.

She said, "Suppose a robot does something well, it gets a reward. If he doesn't do well, it gets punishment." I was bewildered. "That sounds easy. But how exactly does the learning work?" I was thinking all the things we have to teach and whether this was feasible. She said, "The beautiful part of this learning is that the robot doesn't need humans to teach it specific things. It can learn by trying." I was still puzzled.

Seeing my puzzled face, she said, "My advisor is here. Why don't you talk to him tomorrow? I will introduce you to him. His name is Richard Sutton." At the mentioning of her advisor, she seemed more confident. The Doina offered, "Do you know he is the most famous person in this field?" I shook my head, and Doina was firm that I needed to meet her advisor.

The next morning Doina and I came to the lounge area of the dorm. This is when I met Richard Sutton.

"Hi, Rich, I want to introduce you to Junling." Doina called out to him. "She is doing her PhD at University of Michigan, and she wants to know more about reinforcement learning."

Richard Sutton was very friendly. He sat me down on sofa, and pulled out a pad of paper. He started his explanation by writing down equations after equations of this mysterious thing called temporal difference. I tried to follow his logic, but didn't get it. Rich was very patient. Seeing that I was puzzled, he wrote down more equations. That conversation lasted for more than an hour.

The next day, I bumped into Rich again, and I asked him another question. He sat down with me and explained for another hour, this time with more equations and drawings of a game called backgammon (which I never heard of before). I didn't quite understand then, but I was infected by his enthusiasm. Leaving the conference, I started to explore reinforcement learning and even played a few backgammon games. One year later, I wrote a paper on reinforcement learning (for multiagent systems) and focused my PhD dissertation on reinforcement learning.

***

Still, reinforcement learning in the late 1990s and early 2000s was considered impractical. The computing power was not there, and we didn't know how to handle large state space.

In 1998, Richard Sutton published the book *Reinforcement Learning*, co-authored with his advisor Andrew Barton. This book has become the classic book on reinforcement learning. The same year, Sutton joined AT&T Lab. This is a leading research lab that offers AI researchers freedom to explore.

Sutton's book has gained popularity. In 2003, he joined University of Alberta as a professor. The same year, Michael Bowling, a reinforcement learning researcher graduating from CMU, also became faculty at University of Alberta. Together with another well-known reinforcement learning researcher in Sutton's group, University of Alberta had thus become the hub of reinforcement learning.

## Edmonton, Alberta, 2004

A new PhD student arrived at Sutton's office. His name was David Silver. Silver came from the UK. He had built a successful video game startup, but he was very interested in AI and wanted to become an AI researcher. He likes reinforcement learning and wanted to join Sutton's group. Silver became Sutton's PhD student.

Silver had always been fascinated by the game Go. Go is fascinating to researchers because it seems impossible to solve by brute force computing. The possible number of actions for each player is about 361 (19 x 19). The state is the combination of board positions. There are 361 (which is equivalent to 10768 ) possible board positions. This is larger than the total number of atoms in the universe. The method of searching for all possible scenarios to play against based on the current move is just impossible.

In 2008, Silver wrote a computer program that played Go on a 9 x 9 board. The computing power was not there, deep learning was not yet known to most researchers, but Silver's attempt on Go was still amazing. He got the Nectar Award at the AAAI conference in 2008.

\*\*\*

I remembered passing by AAAI demo area in 2008, where there was a big screen showing a Go game board. The speaker (Silver) explained how difficult the game of Gowas. There was excitement and optimism among the listeners. It was so palpable in the air.

Such excitement and optimism is what I felt every time I've attended an AI conference. Researcher after researcher proposes new algorithms and solutions to tackle difficult problems, those we used to think were unsolvable. In the late 1990s, I saw small robots running around at the AAAI conference tournament. Later these robots' incarnation appeared in Roomba and Kiva's warehouse robots. "If you can dream it, you can make it." This seems be the motto among AI researchers.

\*\*\*

The Achille's heel of reinforcement learning is precisely a large state space. How can we record this many possible states and act on them? Researchers have tried many ways, such as "state summary" where you try to use a few patterns. But this is very manual, and you don't know if the patterns you use are, in fact, complete (exhaustive). This is very similar to feature engineering in traditional machine learning, where you try to come up with good features to summarize the data to reduce the input dimensions.

Another approach to the large state space is using so-called "hierarchical state space." You try to use a few high-level states to enumerate possible scenarios, and then move to lower-level states. Again, how do you build such a hierarchy that is manual and prone to errors?

Researchers in reinforcement learning were struggling with the solution to handle large state spaces. It was the reason that I got frustrated and left the research field of reinforcement learning. But many others persisted. Sutton has never given up on finding a solution.

Silver graduated in 2009 and went back to the UK. He continued his work on Go. But first, he wanted to improve reinforcement learning to handle large numbers of actions and state space. It was not until deep learning became popular after 2012 that he found a natural ally to help in this endeavor.

At this time Silver joined his friend Demis Hassabis's new startup called DeepMind. They both loved games and wanted to build AI systems into games.

# 15.

## Deep Reinforcement Learning: Behind AlphaGo

**London, UK, 2013**

David Silver was glad to see a new employee at DeepMind, Volodymyr Mnih, who was his old schoolmate at U. Alberta (who pursued a master's degree then). Mnih later moved to University of Toronto to study for a PhD degree in Geoff Hinton's group. Now Mnih had graduated and was been well-versed in deep learning with the training from Hinton.

Mihn was a natural partner for Silver when Silver thought of the next place to apply reinforcement learning. "At least we can start from a computer game," Silver proposed. What game is easy to program? They picked Atari games. The games were arcade video games, with very simple pixels. These games go back to the 1970s. Steve Jobs was once an Atari game programmer.

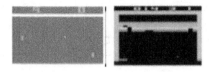

Figure 15.1: Two Atari Games: Pong (Left) and Breakout (Right)

In the Atari games, you have simple actions – up, down, left, right. Bu the possible states are large. Each state is the position of the ball, which may jump in unexpected directions. A player receives a reward when they win the game.

How do we build an AI agent to play this game? For every situation, the agent needs to decide what action to take. The state can be captured by the video picture frame. Each picture frame can be processed by a convolutional neural network. The output of this neural network is the Q-value of four different actions. In other word, we are learning the Q-value associated with actions for every state.

The neural network starts without knowing anything about the states and best actions, and gradually learns through observing its reward. Q-value captures the long-term reward.

They call this method deep Q-learning, where one uses a deep neural network (such as CNN) to learn Q-values.

More generally, they have successfully combined deep learning with reinforcement learning, which enables an agent to learn optimal actions in complex situations. They coined the term deep reinforcement learning for this new method. A new field was born.

146

Their paper was presented at NIPS 2013, and later published in *Nature* in 2015.

## AlphaGo

With the success in Atari games, David Silver had gained the confidence to pursue Go. In 2014, the AlphaGo team was formed. By now, DeepMind had been acquired by Google (in January 2014). Suddenly, all the computing resources from Google were available to them. They were no longer a small startup. This also enabled them to get help from researchers inside Google. Ilya Sutskever, now working in Google Brain, had come to DeepMind to help on AlphaGo design.

The game Go is both similar to and different from an Atari game. It's similar to an Atari game in that you can capture the complex board position as a picture, like the video picture framework for a video game. This allows you to take advantage of a convolution neural network, which does an excellent job in summarizing an image, and mapping it to the right category.

AlphaGo treats the board patterns by treating them as pictures. A board picture is divided into 19 by 19 regions. We can then apply a convolutional neural network to this picture. In each layer, we take subregions to learn. Each layer feeds into the next layer, and we are learning an overall representation of the whole board. The output of this CNN is the actions or moves of the AI player. There are 361 possible actions or 361 outputs (the actual legal moves could be smaller).

Here we directly learn the best action in each state without learning the Q-values. This network is thus called a "policy network." A policy refers to a sequence of actions that leads to the final outcome. AlphaGo uses a policy network instead of deep Q-learning (used in Atari games).

Figure 15.2: AlphaGo's policy network

In the above figure, the input layer is at the bottom and it is the current board position (indicated as *s*), the top layer is the output layer, giving the probabilities of different actions. In Go, the action is equivalent to the location on the board (to put down the next stone).

AlphaGo uses a 13-layer convolutional neural network for the policy network. It trains this network in two ways. One is using supervised learning by matching human moves for 30 million positions in a Go play database (KGS Go server). Another way is it uses reinforcement learning by playing against itself. It receives reward 1 for winning, -1 for losing, and 0 for neither winning nor losing. It does self-training millions of times.

In addition to the policy network, AlphaGo also learns a value network, which maps the board position to its final value (positive if winning and negative if losing).

The Go game is different from Atari games in that you are playing against an intelligent player (not just a dot that is bouncing back). Thus, it is much more complex. For games with opponents, we can use a tree search to evaluate current moves against the opponent's all possible moves.

In chess, a game tree expands all possible moves against another player, and goes deeper to the end of the game (when one person wins). This expanding strategy does not work for AlphaGo, as there are too many possible situations. For this reason, AI researchers were pessimistic that we would ever create a Go program that wins. Even it was possible, people thought it would be in another decade.

AlphaGo resolved this complexity by avoiding expansion on all possible moves. It only selected the best move based on the results from its policy network and value network. Thus, computation is significantly reduced.

From the best move, Alpha expands deeper into future moves. It repeats this same expansion but each time, it randomly samples possible moves from the opponent to get the average results. This is called the Monte Carlo method. Monte Carlo is a casino in Monaco where people gamble and take chances. In statistics, the Monte Carlo method refers to taking random samples repeatedly and getting the average of the samples as the true value. Combining tree search with the Monte Carlo methods, we allow faster searches for evaluating a move. This makes AlphaGo much more efficient. The winning is not based on an exhaustive search any more. This method was dubbed by the AlphaGo team the Monte Carlo Tree Search.

In 2015, AlphaGo defeated the European champion. In March 2016, in a worldwide real-time broadcast, AlphaGo defeated 18-time world champion Lee Sedol in Seoul. Many could not believe it, such a complex ancient game, whose top player is the pride of a nation, could be defeated by a computer. Some were scared. Could AI be really so powerful? Some argued that maybe it was just a fluke.

All the dust was settled when AlphaGo was undefeated 60-0 against top human players online, and 3-0 against the world's number one player, Ke Jie in China.

The success of AlphaGo came from the combination of two powerful machine learning methods: deep learning and reinforcement learning. Reinforcement learning enables an agent to act and observe the long-term payoff, deep learning enables the agent to process the situation faster, more accurately.

After AlphaGo, we are seeing several breakthroughs. One is Deep Mind's AlphaZero, which extends beyond the AlphaGo algorithm from Go to chess and other board games. It turns out there is no need to create specialized training on a type of game. A general purpose algorithm uses generic state-action representation and encoded game move

150

constraint, and can output the specialized algorithm. Deep reinforcement learning is now moving toward the practical world (still in board games, though).

The second domain is video games, where the position of opponents and the game situation can be summarized in images. Thus, CNN is very powerful to represent states and pass that information to the action learning in RL. From Atari games to driving games, OpenAI has released more than 100 games where you can introduce deep reinforcement learning agents.

The third domain is robotic control. This is just taking the simulation to the real world. Robots learn to move and manipulate an object (such as moving its arm to interact with the object). It certainly depends on image recognition, but also depends on a sequence of movements.

We also see applications in autonomous driving, where the action of a driver is limited. You can consider an autonomous car a robot, one which is reacting to sensor inputs (in terms of images), and deciding to move forward, left, or right, or stop. The speed can be considered another action too.

In late 2017, David Silver came back to Edmonton, Alberta. For him, this was a trip full of memory. Silver met with his advisor Richard Sutton and another professor Michael Bowling. He convinced them DeepMind needed their help.

In 2017, Richard Sutton joined DeepMind. In the same year, Doina Precup became Head of Deep Mind's office in Montreal.

The Age of Deep Reinforcement Learning was arriving.

# 16.

## The Bionic Body

Helen Keller longed to see with her eyes. Being both blind and deaf since a young age, she was condemned to a world of darkness, no light, and no sound. With her extraordinary willpower she went through college and became an educator. But Helen Keller missed the things that normal people have, "If I can see just for 3 days," She wrote, "I would long to see people around me, and every detail in my home. I would see the flowers, the leaves and birch."

Today, Keller's dream may come true. This is called bionic eyes. Our natural eyes are essentially optic devices. It receives light signal and send that signal to the brain. Below is the picture of seeing:

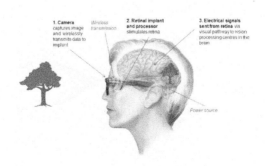

The bionic eye - how it works

1. Camera captures image and wirelessly transmits data to implant

Wireless transmission

2. Retinal implant and processor stimulates retina

3. Electrical signals sent from retina via visual pathway to vision processing centres in the brain

Power source

Figure 16.1: An illustration of how bionic eyes work

The actual processing is taking the light signal and convert that into pixels on a sensor chip.

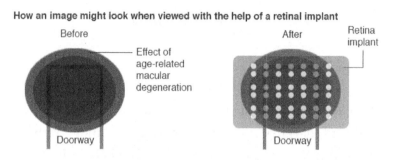

Figure 16.2: An image pattern in the brain

There are two major parts that can be damaged that leads to blindness. The first area is the eye itself. If the eye or the muscle around eyes are damaged, the optic signal cannot come in. As people get older, their eye can degenerate, leading to glaucoma.

The second area is the brain region that processes visual signals. If this region is damaged, a person will lose the ability to see even if the eyes are perfectly normal. Stroke patients can become blind when the blood clot forms in the visual region of the brain.

The bionic eyes can simulate both eye function and brain function. If it is the problem with eye muscle, we can implant a tiny camera in our eyes. The optic signal from the camera will then send to a chip that translates those signals to electronic signals and connects to the brain.

Today such devices are implanted for older people who have degenerated eyes, this saves them from blindness.

For people who became blind due to brain injury or stroke, we can use a computer chip in the brain to receive a signal from an implanted camera (at the eye area). This chip has the processing power that is fast enough for coming images. We can make this chip directly communicate with the eye region or with a camera that we process.

How does AI help? Eventually we need quick imaging processing on the chip and trigger the brain to react. This same thing goes to chips that detect and process sound.

Today's deaf people already enjoy a device called cochlear Ear. It implants a speech processor in the ear, which converts the sound to electric signal that stimulates the cochlear nerve, causing it to send signals to the brain. Deafness is cured. If Keller lived to today, how happy she would be.

Taking one step further, can we simply have a chip that receives a word, and immediately trigger our language region? In other words, we can learn new words without memorizing them. Suppose we know 1 language, English. If we can insert into the brain thousands of pairs of words from the English and Italian languages, then we could possibly detect the meaning of new words of the other language.

In movie Robocop (2014), a policeman was injured after a car bomb. He lost arms and legs. The doctor equipped him with bionic arms and legs, which he can control with his thoughts. He wore glasses that retrieve information and can match people to a criminal database.

Imagine that one day you can control your hand even if you are totally disabled from the waist down. All the disabilities will no longer exist. The paralyzed can stand and walk, using their thoughts to control their artificial legs.

We are at the dawn of miracles that have never been seen in human history. The human existence will be transformed as we move beyond the limitation of our biological body.

# 17.

## Summary: The AI Evolution

The life of AI was conceived in 1936 when Turing invented computers. The existence of Ai owes to the computer that provides it with a body and a brain. Building AI is essentially an engineering feat. It's "nuts and bolts," writing coding for its brain.

But AI as a new born was delivered only 20 years later in 1956, coming into this world with its cries and shouts. It has been delivered, nourished, and raised by 4 parents.

AI stayed as an infant for almost 30 years, until 1986. By then, he starts to walk and stumble around. He is fed with good nutritious food (data), and he can talk and see. His ability is limited, but he is eager to learn. The teaching and education of AI has been a bumpy road.

It takes another 26 years, until 2012, for AI to grow up. Now, he can run. He's gaining ability and he can run faster each day.

The evolution of AI is a process of trial and errors. There were high hopes and then disappointments. Neural networks appeared in 1957, but was quickly shot down and went into hibernation.

Rule-based systems got a lot of excitement in the beginning, but reached its limitation in 1990s when the Internet started.

AI development is corresponding to the development of computer, particularly the computing power. It is also related to data, which makes machine learning possible.

Among all AI systems, we see a steady growth of neural network. First, it was very slow then it picked up speed and now it's accelerating. This is the system that is trying to mimic the human brain, and letting nature takes its course (self-updating, raw picture input). The field is now called deep learning, which references the fact there are now being more layers in the network.

The Internet makes available huge amount of data, which make machine learning methods flourish. Many machine learning methods were invented in in this era. But they come and go. Eventually they will die out.

As of today (2019), only remnants of the rule-based system remain. Shallow machine learning is still widely used but it will soon be overpassed by deep learning (in 2-3 years). Given the exponential growth of deep learning applications, I expect that in 10 years, around 2030, neural network-based method (deep learning) will be the only AI system left. It's a tipping point and when the singularity happens.

Reinforcement learning is newer and now is used together with deep learning. It will grow together with deep learning. This can be seen the figure below.

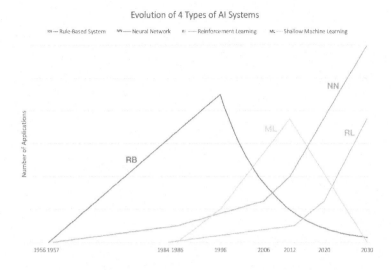

Figure 17.1: The growth of 4 types of AI systems

The future belongs to deep learning and reinforcement learning.

The real insight we learned here is that AI is not a perfect design for the beginning. While humans created AI in their image (like God created human in his image, just an analogy), we are giving AI systems the freedom to learn, to adapt, and to explore. Would an AI system grow to have consciousness? This remains an open question.

# 18.

## The Future

### A Day in the Future

I wake up to my favorite piano music. It is 5 am. The light automatically turns on in the room. A pleasant female voice comes across the room, "Good morning, Junling. It's 5 o'clock on Friday, April 19." Feeling a little sleepy, I habitually say, "Thank you," and pull myself out of the bed.

As I sit at the edge of my bed, the program senses my movement out of bed, then proceeds to talk, "Junling, would you like to hear your schedule for today?" "Yes, go ahead," I grunt when I start to move around.

A car comes to my house. I have scheduled it to come at 8 am every weekday morning. I don't have to worry about it, and it is always there at 8 am. As I step into the car, there is no driver. I sit down in the front row. Now there is no separation between driver and passenger. The car has two rows, and very much resembles a sedan, but with bench seats.

The car greets me with a pleasant female voice: "Good morning, Junling." "Good morning," I speak back, settling in my seat. The door closes, and the car heads to my company, located just ten miles away.

"We are 15 minutes from destination based on current traffic," the car announces. I listen.

The car is Internet connected and can launch my home Alexa system. All personal apps are automatically connected to this car the moment I step in, which includes my home assistant Alexa.

On the road, it stops at a traffic light, waits for the green light, then restarts smoothly.

I see many autonomous cars on the road, almost half of these cars are without drivers. There are two lanes dedicated to such cars. They are allowed faster speeds. These cars are classified to be green since they are universally electric. In addition, they are mostly used for taxi services taking people between home and work. They are very easy to call as there is always one such car nearby.

My car pulls up to my company front door. I step out of the car, and the car says, "Goodbye." I say, "Bye." Then the car leaves by itself.

There are no more big parking lots in front of our company nowadays. In fact, everyone is encouraged to take autonomous cars for commuting to work. The government imposes a fee on using the parking lot at a company. For people who don't want to pay for such a fee, who are reluctant to use the autonomous cars, there is a very small parking lot. The old parking lot is replaced by rows of trees, and flowers. We live in a very green place.

The company building has solar panels on its rooftop, and it seems every company has transitioned to solar-powered rooftops.

There is no longer a receptionist at the door. "Hello," I say. The door recognizes me as I approach. It scans my body gesture, my iris, and my voice.

My first meeting in the morning is with the remote team in New York City. I walk into the virtual reality room. It greets me: "Junling, where would you like to have the meeting?" "New York Office three," I say. "One moment." I stand in the center of the room, and put on the goggles and the gloves with wireless sensors.

Within a second, the room changes into a breathtaking view. One side is a large glass window, going from ceiling to the floor, overlooking a beautiful ocean. There is a big oval shaped desk in the center, like in any conference room. I see John and Don who are already inside the room, chatting. They are my colleagues in New York. They smile and wave at me as I walk in. The seaside scene makes this room so calming. I feel like I'm stepping into an offsite resort, enjoying the time away from the city. Feeling energized, I start our meeting.

\*\*\*

The future is so palpable. It's right here. Uber just announced that it will deploy flying taxis. Drones have been helping construction companies track building progress and farmers with reviewing crops.

What will the Future Look Like? Here are some of my predictions:

## Autonomous Cars and Drones

In the near future, autonomous cars will become common. A few decades later, no one will have a car at home anymore. When you need a car, you can request a self-driving car from your phone. This car is parked in a city parking hub located just five minutes away from your home. There are many in a city hub that enables fast delivery to the nearest resident.

Parking lots will be a thing of the past. Instead, all the cars are concentrated in the central delivery hub. For people who are rich, they have dedicated car in the hub or parked at home. Most people simply request a car when they need it. Once they reach a destination, the car leaves. They can reserve and pre-schedule the car. The scheduling software thus becomes a big business, along with car rentals.

Car accidents and death from car accidents will be greatly reduced. All the autonomous cars drive within a fixed distance of each other. They change lanes to optimize distance and time. They can anticipate obstacles and stop ahead of time. Riding in a car is very safe for humans.

Finally humans are liberated from driving, a mentally taxing, and wasteful activity.

For privacy, you can choose to not broadcast your car location to others. The car rental company would set a strict policy for their employees not to look at your location, just as today's Dropbox promises not to look at your file.

## Employment

When manufacturing jobs and car driving jobs disappear, where do people go? They become knowledge workers. The majority of them move into computer programming. After all, we need more computer engineers to program new routines, to debug, and to test. Computer engineers become the new factory worker in an age where our products carry programs (intelligence) in them: our doorbells, cookware, refrigerators, cars, the store glass doors (that display ads to you). In other words, the Internet of things calls for more programming skill. The actual manufacturing of this hardware is all delegated to industrial robots.

People (who are highly creative) are free from menial work: cooking, driving, housecleaning. All of these are handled by robots or a delivery system managed by robots. People now enjoy a frictionless life. There is more demand for data scientists, who handle the scheduling of autonomous cars, making the most efficient use of their allocation, who mine patterns from the vast amount of data collected from devices, and give relevant help. Personalization is everywhere.

The more intelligent our devices become, the more the demand for data scientists increases. That's because making sense of data and building more intelligent capabilities is extremely important for every product. I believe there will be at least 1 million new data scientists in the next decade.

Virtual reality becomes a main form of interaction with the world. A large number of people will move into creating goods in this virtual world: virtual houses, avatars, virtual clothes, and virtual streets. All the artists now have to learn programming in order to find job in this virtual world. We will see a big transformation of virtual art professions. Maybe they will work next to programmers, but they need to be comfortable with the computer and virtual reality world. Their work is rendered in there. The demand for artists will increase as we will see a gold rush toward building frontier real estate in the virtual world.

We will interact more with each other in the virtual world, which reduces travel. Future meetings will be conducted in 3-D virtual meeting rooms, and your body is rendered as almost real. There is a camera (scanner) that captures your full-body in real-time, and immediately puts you into that meeting room. You wear glasses that allow you to enter that virtual room. When you call from California, your colleague in New York answers, and appears to sit at one side of the table, and another colleague in London also sits at the other side. You can walk around and even shake hands with them. What's rendered in that virtual world is full-size duplicates of people, as today you see in video camera in 2-D fashion. You will wear a glove that connects to that 3-D world. As your eyes and hands are fully engaged, your voice is transmitted in real-time. What about facial expression? How to render them if we want the person to wear glasses? All of these exciting challenges call for engineers and entrepreneurs. There are new jobs being created in this domain.

Human creativity is freed as all the menial jobs are done by robots (or intelligent programs). There are new frontiers to tackle. How to build more bionic body parts? The bionic part companies will create more jobs, demanding more computer programmers, and data scientists. They also need mechanical engineers.

There will be more fitness trainers and sport coaches. As people gain more free time, they have more need for recreation and exercise. There will be more personal coaches and life coaches too. The once elite industry now opens up to more people. In fact, a new platform will be created for people to coach and teach each other. It's an Airbnb system for talents. Trust and credentials are required, but the sharing of personal experiences and coaching each other becomes a service you can provide.

Online dating will be transformed by virtual meeting rooms, as you can easily meet a date in a virtual restaurant and figure out whether you two are compatible.

The travel industry will continue to boom, as people are freed from drudgery of daily life and gain more vacation time.

The land on the earth is still limited, therefore we will see more high rise buildings and rising price of real estate. Flying taxis (drones) will become more common. They will deliver goods and take people to their destinations. This means more people going into designing and programming to maintain these drones. Architects will still be in demand for buildings and new landscapes.

A new space age will begin as people migrate to the moon and Mars. More people will be employed into the space industry. These are rocket scientists (physicists), mechanical engineers, chemists (for fuel study), and computer engineers.

Scientists, engineers, artists, and entertainers will be the main professions of the future. Gone are the blue-collar jobs, and many white-collar jobs (the job of a secretary, such as scheduling and email drafting can be done by a computer). We will have entered the age of pure intelligence and individuality. More and more people will get master's degrees and PhD degrees. Today's people need a bachelor's degree to get a decent job, jobs in the future will require a minimum of a master's degree. Education will become all the more important, and lifetime education is a must.

In the transition, people who are not educated or lack motivation to receive more education will experience the pain of job loss. The employment strategy for these people must focus on education. It is no longer "job training" to fill in some blue-collar or white-collar job, we must give them skills to become knowledge workers. In other words, the displaced workers should get at least a bachelor or master's degree before re-entering the job market. They can also learn computer programming in a few months, and get to work right away. To be clear, the easiest job to get and to train for is computer programming. This is the blue-collar job for the future. Mastering a programming language is like mastering a language to speak to the computer, except now this language requires a lot of logic thinking and clear debugging skill. Therefore, all the future trainees should take discrete mathematics to sharpen their understanding.

Basic math and basic programming should be required for all college classes. This will lay the foundation for people to interact with the computers.

## The Bionic Race

In the near future, we will see rapid development of bionic limbs, as this helps a lot of people with limb loss (2 million people are living with limb loss in the US today). Technology that enhances such devices will also come along: lighter material for limbs, artificial skin. Batteries supporting implants will get smaller and smaller, some could even be implanted into the skin.

In addition, we will see brain implants that dramatically enhance the brain's reaction. As we understand more about the brain, with the development of neuroscience, we can even implant precisely into the brain the signal we want, such as the signals to control the limbs.

In addition, we can implant new knowledge into the brain, such as English words in the form of dictionaries. When this kind of implant becomes possible, we can dramatically change our human capability. Gone will be the days of memorizing a lot of facts. There is the question of whether our new knowledge can integrate with our old knowledge and old experiences. Or if there is a region of our brain that is automatic and separated from other regions. It's possible as this could be a locomotive skill, or music skill. This could be visual memory that has nothing to do with understanding. Once this is done, we are taking a big step toward the bionic body.

The brain implant for the blind has a lot of implications. When we can completely cure blindness through artificial eyes, we will make big progress on brain understanding and implants. This will jump-start all bionic parts, from limbs to facial muscles, to vocal cord. Very soon, we can repair a damaged human body through these electronic devices and the person will be back to normal (the flesh materials could come from stem cells, growing into limbs or organs, but electrodes are implanted into these fleshes.) Disabled persons will walk around with legs or arms (covered with artificial skin) much like able-bodied persons, and they can claim a normal life. They can run or ski, as the artificial limbs work seamlessly with the other parts of the body. How much benefit AI can bring the quality of life?!

Then we will see cheating in sports as some people may extend their legs by replacing human legs with artificial legs, or simply hire people with artificial legs as they run faster. The bionic body gives people more power. Very soon disabled people with artificial limbs will be allowed into competition with able-bodied athletes, and compete at the same level or better. We will reach a threshold when mechanical parts become cool. They will look soft and be agile, while our flesh bodies will look dumb and slow.

This will also completely disrupt cosmetic surgery, as we can easily put on artificial skin to look perfectly beautiful. In that time, everyone will look perfectly beautiful and young.

Taking one step further, there will be leg extensions for ballet dancers, simply by adding a segment of leg between the knee and the hamstring. For ballet dancers, this could be a sacrifice worth having. Wouldn't this be similarly attractive for basketball players?

Society will erupt into two types of people, bionic and natural. Given their implants, bionic people will be stronger and more agile. But they want to participate in social activities such as sports, entertainment shows, and other activities. Over time, the bionic people will want equal rights to the natural people. This may change the rules of the sports and entertainment industries.

## Medicine

In the near future, personalized medicine will save countless lives, creating cures for cancers. Our life spans will expand. In addition, more trained doctors will specialize in eyesight correction, new cosmetics, and aging related research.

## The Future Robots

In the next decade, there will be rapid development of humanoids. The development of bionic parts lends its material to the robotic body. Our robot now has normal skin (artificial) and normal limbs. They walk agilely and they look beautiful.

Robots will have a very agile body. They move around helping elderly people, walking the dogs, and carrying dishes in restaurants. They will become part of our everyday life, ever more helpful, and ever more docile.

In the beginning, these robots will be limited to certain roles: a sex companion, a child, or a maid. These robots will get smarter and smarter with regard to their brain function. Their human master will forget that they are not humans and start to project emotion onto them. The scenes in the movie *A.I.* are not far away. They will come in a box, activated by us. Then they will start to walk around the house like your normal companions. When you don't want them, you can simply say, "go rest yourself," and they will simply go away and sit in a corner. You can activate them by simply calling their name, like how we call Amazon's Alexa today. These robots are so serene and docile that you think they are better than a real person, where as a real person may argue with you and has unstable behaviors.

The story in Asimov's novel when a mother prefers the robot child over the real child is not far away. In her mind, this robot child is her real child too.

A lonely and vain bachelor man will want to take his beautiful robot "girlfriend" to dinner or parties. These robots could make conversation almost like a human being. She smiles beautifully (given the advance of artificial face), and she is quick and witty. She has good behavior and is always understanding. Very soon, we will look at this stunning, beautiful woman at the party: Is she a real person or a robot?

We will inject emotions like love and bonding onto robots. As they become emotional (or show emotional capabilities), the human master will develop deeper bonds with these robots. This is like today we have deep bonds with our pets. These robots can talk and give your real comfort (even sexual). How can a person not fall in love with them? They have infinite time and patience with you. They can talk to you about any subject. An entrepreneur can use them as a sounding board. A housewife can use them as a confidant.

We can also program personality into robots, making them humorous, or more joyful, or more mellow.

Upgrades on these robots will be done remotely, as all data for these robots will be stored in the cloud. Could someone hack into those remote servers and unleash a virus? Could one night all the robots exhibit violent behavior? This is totally possible. This could be prevented by installing safety features on the robot, such as Asimov's laws. Thus, a household robot can never harm a human being. These safety instructions could never be overwritten. However, sinister instructions could be given to the robot to unplug the household electricity or the Internet, or lock the humans inside the house. There are many ways a robot can create harm once it is inside the house. Should we be fearful?

Like every virus, the good people will fight back and eradicate the virus, but now the damage is to physical human bodies and it is much more devastating and widespread. Some people start to become very fearful of robots, and anti-robot society will spring up. Lynching (or killing) of robots will be a new social phenomenon. By that time, people who hold a benign view of robots and who are optimistic of technology containment will argue for the rights of robots. It's like today's rights for a dog killed by a neighbor. Robots will gain rights because of the emotional attachment of their masters.

## Our Home

What will our home look like then? You entered the door that recognizes your face and your fingerprint. Or it simply knows your phone and unlocks for you as you approach. The door opens by itself, you enter a house that has an intelligent thermostat that knows many things about you. The light turns on, switching to "host at home" mode. The music turns on, which is your favorite piano music. Your home robot (mobile or sitting in your living room) greets you, "Hello, welcome home." Even though there are four people in this house (you, your spouse, and your two children), the robot recognizes you through the information from the door. That door is linked to a central server in this house, which is then linked to the cloud for general intelligence. You speak back to the robot, which has the cute name Julo. "What would be for dinner tonight?" The robot is in charge of planning out a different dinner menu each day, and can order meals through a local restaurants. The food is then delivered a short time after you arrive home. Julo reads out the menu to you: "Today the family dinner will be ..."

Your robot remembers each family member's preference, for example the husband likes seafood, particularly sea bass. The two children love egg dishes, preferably with tomato. The wife is a strict vegetarian and likes lentil soup. For the week, Julo changes menus, but essentially settles down on a few dishes that everyone likes. She also creates some surprise dishes that delight the family.

Cloud-managed contact becomes a norm and we no longer bother with a phone any more. Instead, we have a powerful watch that has our information, we talk to devices that are all Internet connected. Our speaker (like Amazon Echo) can retrieve our contacts or schedules, our TVs can make a call for us, and our robot can read for us or conduct a call for us. All of these devices can access our account in the cloud.

## Home Assistant

Alexa becomes proactive. Alexa does not have to wait for us to call her. She can simply take a proactive approach, "Hello, Junling, it's your scheduled reading time. I am reading your book from Audible."

She starts to make active recommendations:

"Here are Audible books read by people like you, would you like to listen to a sample?"

"Here is music liked by other people, would you like to listen?"

Alexa has become a real personal assistant. She can listen to my email dictation and send out email on behalf of me.

She can also schedule my day when other people request meetings.

Alexa has had a body makeover. She comes in an ear piece what connects to my phone with Bluetooth. Nestling behind my ear, she is always listening to me.

I ask her questions when I walk on the street. As she becomes smarter, I talk to her more. "Alexa, I feel a little down today." "Would you like me to cheer you up? How about a joke like this one …" She starts to tell jokes. I chuckle. I know her understanding is limited, but she seems to be trying. The fact is that she tries to understand me and helps to make me feel good.

## Space Travel

Humans have colonized Mars and have settled permanently there. Many people have immigrated there, even though they have to endure more than a year of travel time. The spaceship made it very comfortable for them to pass the time in travel.

## Final Words

We are at the dawn of explosive growth of artificial intelligence. AI, originated from Turing's decisive insights, incubated by Rosenblatt's petri dish, has grown and flourished. She has become a full-fledged being, listening, talking, planning, and helping.

She is growing up to be the companion to our children. She becomes a helper to the elderly. She is an assistant to the executives. She is the guard outside the company. She is our teacher, our friend and our companion.

Where would she end up? How far can we go? The answers to these questions await us and future generations.

# APPENDIX.

## The Training of a Data Scientist

I recognized the young man as he came up to me from the line of people gathered after my lecture. Earlier, he sat on the first row and watched attentively. He looked like a typical engineer you see in the Valley. He hesitated a little, then talked about his current job at a famous company (where I buy my phone from). He has been a software engineer for some years. "But I am excited about AI, and I want to become a data scientist. What should I do? Should I go back to school to get a PhD or master's in AI?" I paused for an answer. I have been asked this question by many young people.

Earlier I had a conversation with a friend who was hiring a data scientist for his team. He asked, "Who should I hire? What qualification should this person have?"

The market is exploding with the job openings for data scientists. Employers cannot hire fast enough. However, job candidates are few. Many friends reached out to me, "Do you know anyone good at computer vision?" or "Do you know anyone who knows NLP?" As AI becomes a key component for almost all new software, the job gap will get bigger for the next 5 years before more trained candidates fill the market.

Due to the technology shift and disappearance of old industries, many people will switch from their current fields (such as physics, biology, or electrical engineering) to AI. Those who received a PhD in these domains have a good start because of their exposure to research methodology and statistical training.

There are two core requirements in a data scientist:

1. Strong Computer Science (CS) training that includes both coding and understanding of computational principles

2. Machine learning training

Writing code is a part of a data scientist's daily job. A data scientist deals with data day in and day out. He is an engineer by nature, and this is hands-on work. A data scientist needs to process a large amount of data. To work with data of 100,000 customers, you need to write code to retrieve their purchase history, converting text data into numerical data that the computer understands. When you deal with the data of 1 million customers, then your computing skill faces bigger challenges. For example, Samsung sells more than 1 million TVs each year, and a sales predictive model would have to process all the data involving every consumer.

Training a machine learning model requires writing code to convert data into the right format, and process all the data together, and train the model with some open-source tool. This means processing millions of rows and getting it done in a short amount of time. A person who lacks CS training would write a code that runs very slowly or would struggle with pulling the data into the system. This involves basic training in the data structure, computer algorithms, and file systems.

Fortunately, there is a whole industry devoted to teaching people coding. This is due to the demand for software engineers in the last 20 years.

Machine learning research refers to being trained as a scientist who can investigate and draw conclusions. How do we teach the machine learning methodology to people who come from these two different backgrounds: 1) Software Engineers 2) Non-CS researchers (PhD or MS in another field).

For software engineers, they need to go through rigorous science training. It is not just knowledge of statistics or machine learning, but also habits of scientific investigation. This typically comes from PhD level training. What does a PhD degree give us? There is a fundamental requirement of writing a dissertation in these degree programs. It's a way to analyze the problems we face, to formulate a hypothesis, and to test that hypothesis. Taking a few online classes do not give us that ability. Doing projects does not fully give us that ability either. However, writing a dissertation is the key to critical thinking and scientific investigating. This process is building "intelligence" in a person's approach. Only such a person can be called a "scientist." A PhD's training goes deeper. It creates certain rigors that we only see in scientists.

We are soon going to see an expansion of PhD programs around AI at major universities. Therefore, now is a good time for universities (as businesses that have large enrollment). There is an acute market need for such talents. The enlargement of CS departments in the next five years will be unavoidable; they will overshadow many other departments.

If you cannot get into a university, how can one get the PhD training that is needed? Is it possible to teach critical training to people who are outside the quiet campus and struggle with daily life? What would be such a process?

Group 2, the non-CS researchers, holds the answer to these questions. The most urgent task is teaching them CS fundamentals. It will take about six months (with hands-on projects) for them to be comfortable and versatile in writing code and handling different computing situations. After that, they need to learn the machine learning (ML) methodology. For this group of people, it is relatively easy to pick up critical thinking and investigation. However, they will miss the fact that ML research is an experimental science. The methodology of ML research is slightly different from that of science or the EE discipline. An ML researcher has to design and build their system constantly. They experiment with the design and compare it with the designs of others. Sometimes others don't have their design code available; then the ML researcher has to duplicate that design with their code. This is a process that is both engineering and research. To do such research, a person has to be very familiar with the current state of the art and read much of the literature that comes out relative to the field. This person also has to be hands-on with the coding and quickly iterate the experiment.

A non-CS researcher will go through the learning of an AI PhD program again, with the new exposure to AI methodology and CS coding training. The challenge for them is no less than for the engineers.

The conversion of these two groups of people to data scientists can fill the big market need for PhD AI researchers and scientists. The results are not ideal. This is why CS PhD graduates are in high demand in the market.

How do we facilitate the process of conversion of Group 1 and Group 2? The software engineers need knowledge and rigorous research training, and non-CS researchers need knowledge and experimental training. Many classes fill the knowledge gap. However, how do we teach research to Group 1 and experimental skills to Group 2?

This is a process of learning by doing, and a person has to take on challenging projects and go through the process. This raises the question: How do we train a PhD outside the campus? How do we create a discussion place where all students will come together to discuss and learn? They would join a research group and simply learn from others. This will be the fastest way to learn. We also need advisors who can guide them in research.

Why not utilize all of those who graduated from PhD programs to teach and share their knowledge? This will be a place where people can learn by examples. Alternatively, we can simply have equal size of real CS PhDs and learners. They will do projects together, and the learners will catch up on the thinking process. Unfortunately, there is so much hidden knowledge that the real AI PhD uses that it is invisible to the learner. Through learning by doing, the learner will catch up on that thinking process of the PhD

The following are for those who are interested in enrolling in a PhD program. I want to share a glimpse of what it takes to get a PhD degree.

## What's in an AI PhD Degree?

It takes on average five years to get a PhD in AI. The first two years are classes and the next three years of research. The class part is nothing exceptional. It is a master's degree level training. What's unique about the PhD degree is the next three years after the classes are done. These are years of intensive research, and where a young student morphs into a researcher. This transformation is done through the following three activities:

1. Publishing research papers
2. Interacting in a research group
3. Writing a PhD dissertation

Let's take a look at each of these activities.

### 1. Publishing Research Papers

A computer science PhD student is expected to publish at least three to four papers by the time they graduate. Some people have written 10 or more papers. Such papers are typically published at conferences. (The major machine learning conferences are: NIPS, ICML, ICLR, KDD, and AAAI.)

The paper acceptance rate of a top AI conference is around 20–25%. That means out of 2,000 paper submitted, only 400 are accepted. This fierce competition ensures a standard of excellence in the papers that are published.

To be accepted for publication, a paper has to demonstrate the following properties: (1) Innovation (2) Significance of the problem (3) A feasible solution demonstrated through experimental results (4) Good writing (Clear, concise).

A researcher has to invent. Each research paper proposes a new method that no one has done before. For example, if someone proposed using 12-layer neural networks, you can propose a 14-layer neural network. There is something new in your paper. This requires an inquisitive mind, extensive reading on other people's work, and deep thinking on all possible solutions. You need to demonstrate that your new method works.

A researcher also has to pick an important problem to solve. If you pick a problem that is trivial, your solution is not advancing knowledge. An important problem once solved has a big impact. For example, the paper on residue networks (ResNet) created a neural network of 152 layers. By doing so, they demonstrate that there is a new way of building large neural networks. Their work has since been adopted by all work on computer vision.

Then how do you know which problem is important? You have to review the literature (all previous papers). This forces you to read widely and attend conferences to stay up-to-date. The topic selection reflects an inquisitive mind that can understand what is and what's not feasible.

After designing your solution, you run many experiments on the computer to show that it is superior (if you are lucky) to all the other solutions known so far.

If you are lucky enough to discover a good solution, you will then write a paper. Writing a research paper is putting together your thoughts, constructing a coherent solution, comparing them with the literature, and demonstrating the superiority of your solution. It takes on average three months to finish a good paper, which includes literature review, algorithm design, experiments, and the actual writing.

Finally, you submit your paper for publication, typically to a conference. You then receive feedback from the reviewers. Here is where you will receive sharp opinions, not only on your content but also on your writing. Many times you have to revise your paper so that it is clearer, and the literature review is comprehensive.

Publishing sharpens one's mind and forces a person to work hard, read widely, and explore deeply. A good paper reflects curiosity, good judgment, persistence, and high standard of excellence. (This is why when I interview a data scientist candidate, I like to review their publications.)

Writing a paper involves identifying a problem, designing innovative ways to solve the problem, doing experiments, and presenting the solution coherently. All of these are the required skills of a data scientist in the workplace.

## 2.  Interacting in a Research Group

A PhD student is supervised by one professor, who is the student's academic advisor, financial supporter, and a research partner in writing papers.

Your advisor is your mentor. They demand that you have a rigorous approach to your work. Their high standards push you to higher ground. In weekly meetings with my PhD advisor, I discussed my ideas and got his feedback. I learned to sharpen my research, math skills, and arguments about why my research was innovative. He also gave me idea on how to present and where to look for literature.

A successful professor can get many grants and fund a large group. My advisor used to have ten students in his group. Interacting with others in a research group is a learning ground. You observe how other people do research, how they get papers published, and how they present their ideas. In the weekly group meeting, you get to listen, to discuss, and to share.

A large research group provides a stimulating environment where you are pushed for excellence. When fellow students publish in top conferences, you want to do the same thing. When they do internships at a top research lab, you want to do the same thing. The list goes on and on. When someone graduates and lands a good job, you have something to strive for.

I remember one time a fellow group member came back from his internship at Microsoft research. He presented the idea of a recommender system. This was in the time before Netflix. He talked about user-user similarity and other ways to infer user preference. It was fascinating, but I didn't know where to apply it. Many years later, I led a data science team at PayPal building recommender systems for marketing. It was very easy for me to pick up this topic as the foundation was laid in graduate school.

### 3. Writing a PhD Dissertation

To get a PhD degree, you need to write a dissertation. A PhD dissertation is typically more than 100 pages, requiring much more depth and breadth than a research paper that is merely 10 pages.

The requirements for a PhD dissertation are the same as a research paper in that it shows: (1) innovation (2) the significance of the problem (3) the feasibility of your solution (4) good writing. A dissertation does this on a much larger scale. If writing a paper is like building a small shed, writing a dissertation is building a full house. It takes two to three years to finish a dissertation. It takes hard work and perseverance.

To show that your research is innovative, you have to make sure that nobody has invented the method you are proposing. This requires reviewing all the publications in the world related to your work. This is called a literature review. It typically takes one year to finish the literature review.

By the time you finish the literature review, you are getting clear about your dissertation topic. The topic is a problem you want to solve others have not solved that. Also, you have a vague idea you how you want to solve it.

Deciding on a dissertation topic is a long process. You have to try and experiment. This is where some graduate students give up. How do you demonstrate that your idea is new? This is particularly tricky for students in the social sciences and humanities domains, where it is hard to demonstrate novelty. Many humanities PhD students take six or seven years to graduate.

Fortunately for computer science students, publishing papers train a person to do innovative work. Since each CS PhD student is expected to publish by their second year, they have to swim in the vast ocean of academic water and survive. By publishing papers, they get familiar with research methodology, and how to create new algorithms.

The coherent theme is the real innovation of a dissertation. This is the true value of PhD training, where you can see the whole picture. It is a consistent exploration of one topic. For example, before writing my PhD dissertation, I wrote papers on self-fulfilling bias in a multiagent environment, and I wrote papers on auction agents and how they act by learning about each other. I also experimented with agents playing soccer and wondered what would be their strategies. However, what is the general theme that links these different topics? It's learning in a multiagent environment. Then what is the general theoretic framework that describes the interaction? I remember staying in the library, reading, thinking, and making notes. I remember visiting another department, stumbling on a book on control theory, and discovering the term Markov games. Those were quiet times, with no outside distraction, no obligation. All I had to do was research and study.

Once we settle down on a coherent framework and know that whatever you invent can apply to a large set of problems, the next question is: How to solve this general problem? You provide a new computing algorithm to solve this problem. Here is your unique invention. You demonstrate its soundness with experimental results, along with mathematical proof.

The uniqueness of a computer science PhD vs. other PhD training is the emphasis on computational efficiency. In computer science, we care about time complexity (how long does it take to finish computing?), and space complexity (how much memory space is required to store the data and intermediary results?). We have to show that whatever we invent can be implemented, runs fast, and takes up a reasonably small space.

When you are satisfied with your experimental results, you write up your dissertation. Here, you put all the work together into one piece. As a non-native speaker, I struggled with my English writing then. I remember the red ink on my dissertation marked by my advisor, mostly on grammatical mistakes. It caused much embarrassment for me. Looking back today, it helped me to have a higher standard for fluent writing.

By the time you finish your dissertation, you have endured the lonely graduate life (others already graduated and are working), you have suffered through low-income syndrome as a poor graduate student. You are secluded from the real world, staying in the academic ivory tower, to attack a big problem. It's like a martial arts master who stays inside a mountain practicing his moves; you are practicing the moves in your research thinking and using muscle to attack a difficult problem.

By now your research ability has taken a leap from a year before. You have ascended to a mountain, and you can see the whole horizon of the research field. As a researcher, you have morphed from larvae to a butterfly. You have become an independent thinker.

This is what a PhD training gives you.

\*\*\*

It's a great time to be an AI researcher, engineer, or manager. You are working in a career that will grow in the next decade. The machine learning skill, which applies to many different problems, allows you to switch jobs easily. In one job, you may be working on fraud detection. In the next job, you may work on product recommendation. In one job, you process images, and in the next job, you handle text documents. Mastering machine learning gives you a key to open doors to many magic worlds.

# Acknowledgements

This book could not have happened without the support of people around me. I want to thank my editor Todd Hunter for reviewing and editing. I want to thank Sonia Sharma for research on historical timelines, and Bingyang Wu for reading.

I want to thank my PhD advisor, Michael Wellman, who has opened the door of AI to me. I am especially grateful for Mike's guidance, mentorship, and example of excellence. I want to thank my officemates at University of Michigan and my groupmates, whose discussion inspired me. They made AI fun for me.

I want to thank my sisters and my mother for their unwavering support. They give me unconditional love that sustains me in the up and down of this writing.

I want to thank the people who help to organize the AI Frontiers conference with me, keeping the AI dream going. Particularly, I want to thank Stella Huang who went through the planning and organizing with me, and Apoorv Saxena and Yang Wang for unwavering support in putting the conference together.

I want to thank Len Schubert, who has helped to me to build a chatbot. I want to thank Dekang Lin, who provided support to my startup. I want to thank all my team members at PayPal and Samsung research, their help and support make our delivery possible.

I want to thank Andrew Ng for the research collaboration and for speaking at eBay, and I want to thank my research collaborator Christopher Manning at Stanford University, George Karypis at University of Minnesota, Jiawei Han at University of Illinois at Urbana Champaign.

I want to thank all the people in my life and who help to make AI a dream come true.

# About the Author

Junling Hu is a recipient of the National Science Foundation CAREER award. She has spent the past 20 years leading AI research, product development and public education.

Dr. Hu was chair of the AI Frontiers Conference, which brings together Industrial AI leaders to share the cutting-edge development in AI. She is the Co-founder and CEO of AIPro.io. Dr. Hu was the director of data mining at Samsung Electronics from 2013 to 2015, where she led a team to create intelligent AI products for large-scale recommender systems. Before Samsung, Dr. Hu led a data science team at PayPal, delivering AI solutions for marketing, sales, and customer support and operation improvement. Before joining PayPal, Dr. Hu led a data mining team at eBay, solving problems of large-scale structured and unstructured data. Before joining eBay, Dr. Hu managed a data mining group at Robert Bosch corporation, where she led the data mining effort on large-scale healthcare data and natural language systems.

Dr. Hu was an assistant professor of computer information systems at University of Rochester from 2000 to 2003. Dr. Hu received her PhD in AI from University of Michigan in Ann Arbor.

Website: https://aipro.io

Email: junlinghu@aipro.io

Twitter: @junling_tech